Volume II

CHARITY

True Stories of Giving and Receiving

Edited by
Rosemerry Wahtola Trommer

Red Rock Press   New York

Published by Red Rock Press
459 Columbus Avenue, Suite 114
New York, New York 10024
U.S.A.
www.redrockpress.com

Virtue Victorious angel by Barbara Swanson

Cover Image: Courtney Milne/Masterfile

Back Cover Art: Detail from *Christmas '62* by Thomas Nast

Cover Design by Kathleen Herlihy-Paoli

Book Design by Paul Perlow

TO ERIC AND SHAWNEE

THANK YOU

Alone with my pen
there is nothing. Only when
I remember you
and give in to gratitude,
then the words herd, wild horses come home.

A book about giving and receiving would not be complete without mentioning the glue that links the givers and receivers—gratitude. I am grateful to many people for their assistance in making *Charity* a reality, both directly and indirectly.

Thank you to all of the contributors, for sharing their stories and their words.

Thank you to Ilene and Richard Barth, for trusting me with their brainchild.

Thank you to my husband, for supporting me through this and every endeavor.

Thank you to my mother, who taught me that gratitude is the secret to happiness.

Thank you to my father, who showers me and humbles me with his generosity.

Thank you to my brother, who won't let me get too serious.

Thank you to my grandparents, for giving generations of love.

Thank you to Heartbeat, for letting me sing off some steam.

Thank you to the women of my sacred circle, who have listened to me.

Thank you to Malinda Teel, for your example and advice.

Thank you to Art Goodtimes and Jim Tipton, who teach me humility.

Thank you to Mary Duffy, Karen Metzger, Leila Knox and Michelle Kodis, my wildflower friends, whose love grows and blooms, even when I neglect them.

Thank you to the San Juan Mountains, who are always there.

Thank you to the spirit that connects us all and gives us the gifts we have to give back "in kind."

And reader, thank you for giving your time and receiving these stories. May their charity resonate in you.

—R.W.T.

CHARITY IS LOVE

A neighbor calls on Thanksgiving in tears, then quickly gets off the phone. A woman in the hospital loses too much blood during childbirth and will die without a transfusion. A man stands beside his car at the side of the road, steam billowing from the hood. An old man in a bombed-out village spends his last cent to feed you, a foreigner, a fine dinner.

Each of these situations presents an opportunity for charity. How would you respond? What could you give to help?

"It's not how much we give," said Mother Theresa, "but how much love we put into giving." Her words touch on the intrinsic character of charity. Though charity is commonly associated with giving, at its linguistic root, charity is love. It comes from the Latin word *caritas*, "a love founded on esteem."

This definition leaves no room for pity, only for humble caring. When giving to others, there's a danger of falling into a generous-me-helping-poor-you attitude. True charity requires a me-and-you mindset—a giving relationship based on mutual respect.

To get to this more equalized place sometimes means rethinking what it means to give. Kahlil Gibran offers some insight: "You give but little when you give of your possessions," he says. "It is when you give of yourself that you truly give."

Of course, people need possessions—namely shelter, clothing, food and medicine. But beyond these physical needs are the needs of the human spirit—the need to love and to see oneself as loveable. These needs, so essential to character, can only be met by other human beings giving of themselves.

Humane charity is what this book is all about—giving and receiving on the most personal of levels. It's a book about people responding to each other with genuine kindness and openness. It's about love founded on esteem.

For instance, when *Charity* storyteller Becky Mollenkamp signed up to be a Big Sister, she assumed that she would be "the giver," and her Little Sister would be "the receiver." She wasn't yet open to the possibility that the little girl would have something to offer her. Becky believed her only reward would be the good feeling she got from giving. Luckily, little Marie didn't feel at all confined to the "receiver" role. She treated Becky as her equal, not as her savior. As a result, Becky opened up to receive all the gifts and lessons Marie had for her, too.

Another great example of a giving-receiving exchange is in Tarzie Hart's story of the hobo who came to her grandparents' home for a meal. They put him to work fixing their fence and then served him a lunch on the white tablecloth they reserved for special guests. By giving the hobo a job, not a handout, Tarzie's grandparents allowed for his self-esteem to remain intact. All parties in this exchange are givers, and all are receivers.

But getting something back from the receiver is not the basis for charitable acts. The rewards are often inherent in the very process of giving. For when we open ourselves to being vehicles of kindness, we discover more about who we are, what we have to offer and how we fit into the bigger picture. For instance, in Elizabeth Chase's story about helping an old woman get home, Elizabeth is a reluctant giver. She is late for her job and she is tired. But when she does give the older woman her time and assistance, Elizabeth realizes that she has inherited her father's kindness-at-all-costs ethic. Her charitable response teaches her about who she is, what she believes in and where she comes from.

As in Elizabeth's case, giving isn't always easy. For every reason to give, there are just as many reasons not to. Most of these reasons are fear-based. For instance, John wants to go visit the elderly in the hospice, but he's afraid it will be too hard on him to see their pain. Susie wants to give money to her struggling sister, but she's afraid she doesn't have enough money for her own family. Joaquin wants to help teach a child to read, but he fears he doesn't have enough time to himself as it is. It can seem very difficult to deal with another person's problems when our own needs aren't being met, unless we somehow tap into some half-hidden spring of personal strength.

Another fear is that our skills are inadequate for helping another: You may know a family whose home was destroyed in a mudslide, but you hesitate to help them rebuild their home because you don't know anything about construction. Plus, you rationalize, the Red Cross will do it. Give yourself a chance! Professionals have no monopoly on compassion. And even if it's true that there is nothing you can *do*, you can always just *be* with a person. Sometimes the most important thing you can give is your time, your presence and your willingness to listen.

Perhaps the deepest fear that keeps us from giving is that we, too, could be homeless, hungry, sick or deserted. Of course we could! But often it is the acknowledgement of our vulnerability that allows us to be compassionate and make genuine connections with other people. In Verlie Hutchens' story about a food pantry, the volunteer includes an African violet with the bag of canned goods because experience reminds her that the people who come to the shelter must be starved not only for food, but for beauty, too. To be charitable is to lose our self-defensiveness and open ourselves to being equals with others.

The stories told in this book come from givers and receivers who live in many places. These people are not professional fundraisers or social workers—they're just people talking about actual moments in their lives. Their experiences are the only credentials they need.

As you read these true stories, you may see snippets of your own feelings reflected in the writers' words. Even if you've never been beaten, you can understand physical pain. Even if you've never been estranged from your family, you can understand isolation. This mirror-like property is part of the power of storytelling. Sharing experiences allows us to observe, learn, connect and even heal.

Another mystery inherent in true stories is that they have no definitive beginning. Any starting point is mere convenience. Likewise, true stories have no absolute end. Not only do the people in them move on in their own lives, but the printed story also takes on its own life. You, the reader, ingest these stories and, like the food that you eat, they become part of your constitution. These stories of charity are particularly nourishing. They feed the parts of you that want to be generous.

As you share the authors' experiences, you may notice that in them there are many layers of giving and receiving. There are also many kinds of charity. Is any one kind of giving more important than another? How can you compare a story about a man who loses his life while trying to help others to a poem in which a woman thanks a man who gave her hot water for a bath? How can you compare the gift of education to a blind, deaf and mute girl to the gift of a sentimental car to a husband?

Obviously there are charitable priorities: providing food, shelter, clothing, health care and freedom from oppression. But all of us are called on to be charitable every day in small or large ways. From smiling at the grocery store clerk to lending a long-term hand to someone in distress to writing a generous check to a cause in which you believe, charity has many guises. And you, reader, are uniquely qualified to be charitable—probably in a multitude of ways. What are your gifts? What are your opportunities to forge relationships of love founded on esteem? What is your charity story?

—Rosemerry Wahtola Trommer
Telluride, Colorado

TABLE OF CONTENTS

SECTION I

♦ CIRCLE OF GIVING ♦

Illman Bros.

"Deeds make habits, habits make character, character makes destiny!"
—JANE ADDAMS

STITCHES IN TIME
Kimberly Ripley

Mimi, as I called my great-grandmother, was a member of a Baptist church near her home in Bangor, Maine. My many days spent in her home were among the happiest of my childhood. Within her church a group of elderly ladies had formed a club. Calling themselves The Friendly Circle, they met each week in the 1950s. In addition to enjoying each other's company, they knit mittens, hats, and scarves, crocheted afghans and stitched beautiful handmade quilts for needy folks. Bangor's severe winters necessitated proper winter clothing and blankets—the careful designs Mimi and her friends brought to their work were their added gifts.

Mimi's social life intrigued me as a small child. By the time I arrived she was a widow, and church activities were her social mainstay. "I'll be with The Friendly Circle until four this afternoon," she would tell me right after lunch.

Promptly at 4:10 p.m., her stooped, withered frame would slowly cross the street, having walked home from the First Baptist Church. Her arthritis prevented her from maneuvering as smoothly as she'd have liked. Other ladies offered rides, but she seldom accepted—except on bitter winter days. "If I slip on the ice, I'm a goner," she would admit.

The highlight for The Friendly Circle was their quilting sessions. They began in the spring and continued until early fall. Quilt after colorful quilt was produced lovingly by hand, and Mimi held the record for being the best and the fastest quilter.

In addition to the quilts The Friendly Circle pieced together, my great-grandmother always had more at home she worked on in her spare time. These she would add to The Friendly Circle's collection. "We don't want any little ones going cold this winter," she would say.

The Friendly Circle's list of needy families came from the pastor. He knew the people who needed help within the parish, and the Salvation Army added a few families it could not otherwise provide for. All the families lived in Bangor. Most had several children.

The list the Friendly Circle received each fall detailed the ages and sizes of children in each family. The Circle was to provide a quilt, an afghan and a hat, mitten and scarf set for each youngster.

"What about the adults?" my great-grandmother asked.

"We have to draw the line somewhere," she was told.

Mimi wasn't one for drawing lines.

Night after night she sat in her rocking chair by the window until her eyes no longer could focus and her twisted, swollen fingers no longer could knit or crochet. Working solo, she turned out enough hats, mittens and scarves for all the adults in every

> *"Put yourself in the place of every poor man and deal with him as you would God deal with you."* — John Wesley

family the church was helping.

But this was against the rules. When The Friendly Circle gathered to assemble their packages, Mimi volunteered to do the final packaging each year. Before she wrapped the packages in brown paper and string, she slipped in the extras.

One particular winter that sticks in my mind, the snow piled higher and much earlier than usual. I recall seeing an old black and white photo of me standing next to a snow bank on a shoveled walkway, and the bank was nearly five times my height! It was early November, just about the time of year The Friendly Circle made its deliveries.

A lot of talk had circulated among The Friendly Circle women about a local family with seven children. I'll call them the Cronks. Apparently dirt-poor, with a disabled father and hardly any income, this family was anxious about the rough winter ahead. The Friendly Circle's members were concerned enough to take up a collection among themselves and turn the funds into a check. They tucked their quiet gift into an envelope wrapped inside the package that would be delivered to the Cronks. This was planned on the sly because the ladies of the Circle were not supposed to have extended contact with the people they helped.

The Cronk family's hardship weighed on my great-grandmother, even after she and her friends had planned their extra present. At night when she read her Bible and prayed, she would mention this family to God. She asked how she could be instrumental in easing their suffering.

On distribution day, Mimi once again volunteered to wrap the heavy packages alone. She placed extra hats, mittens and scarves for adults into nearly every package, as was her wont. When she came to the package for the Cronks, my great-grandmother withdrew from her apron pocket a tiny slip of paper. On it was written her name, Mrs. Lillian M. Cole. Her phone number followed. A message was included: "Please let me know how I can help." She slipped the piece of paper deep inside the quilt in the Cronks' package.

She explained to me later that some rules are meant to be broken.

A few days later she got a call.

Mrs. Cronk was overwhelmed with the kindnesses the church had displayed. She was thrilled with the many items her family had been provided. And she was extremely touched by the little note that had been secretly tucked inside.

"Now, you tell me what you folks need," my great-grandmother insisted. She wasn't one to engage in small talk.

Mimi spent the next few days gathering gently-worn clothing. These items had their buttons and zippers removed and their material redesigned into new garments. My great-grandmother kept busy night and day sewing pants, shirts and nightgowns for the Cronk children. She also fashioned an entire wardrobe of baby clothing on her old sewing machine. In addition, she collected cans of coffee, bags of flour and sugar and an entire bin of potatoes. Mimi also let me help her raid her cellar for countless jars of pickles, beets and green beans.

My great-grandmother was determined to see to it that this large family made it through the winter. She enlisted the help of the local Red Cross to provide boots for all the children and the parents, as well. She slipped a few dollars to the old doctor who still made house calls on the understanding that he would visit the Cronks if one of them fell ill. And Mimi telephoned the family daily, bolstering their beaten spirits with encouragement and kindness.

In return for her generosity, my great-grandmother received one of the greatest gifts of her entire lifetime. She gained the friendship of the Cronk family. She considered the trust of the family an answer to her prayers.

The members of The Friendly Circle were never privy to my great-grandmother's little secret. I'm not sure if anyone besides the doctor and me had an inkling of her dedication. However, I do know this: Some rules are, in fact, meant to be broken. The Golden Rule is not among them.

Kimberly Ripley, who lives in Portsmouth, New Hampshire, has written for several publications. A wife and mother of five children, she enjoys volunteering within the school system and is active in her church.

LITTLE SISTER, BIG LESSON
Becky Mollenkamp

I tapped my fingers nervously on the table in front of me. It was a Thursday evening in February, a night usually reserved for watching television. Instead, I was sitting alone on a cold Missouri evening in a small, five-by-five-foot windowless room waiting for the door to open.

I was about to meet my little sister, "adopted" through the Big Brothers/Big Sisters program. Butterflies had fluttered in my stomach all day. Now I was in the grip of fear. Squirming in my chair, I questioned my decision to become a Big Sister. It was a big commitment. I had agreed to spend four hours each week with this girl for at least one year. I'd already failed pretty miserably with my real sibling, a recovering drug addict with whom I rarely spoke. Why did I think I could do better with this little girl?

Would she like me? Would I like her? What would we have to talk about? What in the world would we do together week after week?

I thought of fleeing the room. Then the door swung open.

A bad year had been drawing to a close when I'd decided to devote a few hours a week to charity. It was not a resolution forged from cheer. I had fallen into a slump, a depression, really. Since I'd left college two years earlier, I'd worked in one unrewarding, entry-level marketing job after another. My boyfriend of five years had made it clear marriage wasn't in our near future. I was overweight and out of shape. Calls from creditors came routinely.

There was something missing in my life, maybe many things. I wondered what was so different in the lives of people who seemed so happy during the holidays. It was the season of giving, and it occurred to me that maybe it would cheer me up to give something to someone who had less than I did. I'd never really gotten involved with anything charitable, but now it made sense. I could fill the void in my life by becoming someone's heroine. Yes, I was being a little selfish, but surely that was okay, as long as I helped someone else in the process.

After a few days of searching for a charity case, I'd found the Big Brothers/Big Sisters program. It provided just what I wanted—the opportunity to become involved with a needy girl and really see what a positive influence I could have on her life. After a month-long application process—including an interview, home visit and training—I got the call. Big Brothers/Big Sisters had paired me with a nine-year-old girl named Marie. I'd been told that Marie had been on the Big Sisters waiting list for nearly a year. Marie had never known her father; her mother worked full-time in customer service, but received government assistance to make ends meet.

Marie's profile was everything I'd hoped for: I felt sorry for her the moment I learned of her existence. I knew I could make a difference to this girl. My dad had left for good when I was only two, so I could sympathize with the pain she surely felt. Before I actually entered our meeting room, I couldn't wait to add sunshine to Marie's bleak life.

A scrawny, blonde, mop-topped nine-year-old girl with sparkling blue eyes bounced into the room. Marie flashed me a crooked smile and then ducked behind her heavy-set mother, who had followed her in.

Then she bobbed out front again. During our short introductory meeting, it became clear that Marie was no shrinking violet. She readily told me about her friends, family and school. She asked me about my life. Without hesitation, she chose bowling as our first activity. Then the meeting was over.

Where was the sad, meek child I'd expected? Marie seemed happy. Marie had exhibited more confidence than I had. At the very least, I'd expected to run the show at our first meeting. After all, I was the one performing the good deed. But it seemed that Marie would never stand for that. This little girl was overwhelming.

I picked up Marie promptly at 2 p.m. for our bowling date. She came to the door in tattered jeans, an old T-shirt and a filthy jean jacket. During our first game, I asked questions. She focused on knocking down the pins. But as the afternoon wore on, she began to warm up to me. So I broached the subject of my absentee father, and waited for her to confess to greatly missing hers. Marie only allowed that once in a while she wondered what he was like.

Once in a while? I had spent more than twenty years wallowing in my self-pity about having no father, and I expected Marie to do the same. But Marie apparently didn't feel sorry for herself on that score. She told me that she'd figured out that she didn't really need her dad because she had her mom, brother, grandparents, aunts, uncles and dozens of cousins. Hers was a family full of love, more than enough to take the place of a missing father. Yes, every once in a while she thought it would be nice to have a dad, too, but his absence was "no big deal."

Marie's positive outlook flowed over into every aspect of her life. When I expressed concern that she was too young to be home alone after school and all day during the summer, she promised that it was also "no big deal." She always locked the door and her nearby grandmother called to check on her regularly.

I knew Marie was making the best she could out of her situation, one that she could not control. But when the Midwest heat became nearly unbearable during the summer months, I feared for her comfort and well-being. Week after week, I stepped out of my air-conditioned car to pick up Marie for our planned activity and was greeted at her front door by a wall of stifling heat. If I'd been the one sweating through the summer, my whining would have never ceased. But Marie just shrugged it off. She didn't mind that her mom couldn't afford air conditioning, she said. Most of the time cooled air only made her too cold.

In the fall, Marie's life was turned upside-down—or so it seemed to me. Her mom had lost her job and now even tiny luxuries had disappeared. But as the months of her mother's unemployment dragged on, Marie remained optimistic. She rarely complained about hardship; she assumed her mother would eventually find a job and things would get better.

When her mother found employment after nearly eight months, Marie brimmed with excitement. "Now I can go to the dentist," she said with glee. I was stunned by her comment; I'd always dreaded those visits as a child. Marie confided that she had never been to a dentist. As proof, she showed me a molar that was black to its core. She couldn't wait to have the cavity filled. I didn't have the heart to tell her that she would be facing more than a simple filling and that she risked losing the rotten tooth altogether. My shock, however, must have been written across my face, because Marie told me not to worry. She brushed her teeth twice a day, and the tooth didn't even hurt. As soon as her mother's new health insurance kicked in, she would be heading to the dentist. Her mother had promised.

I was blown away by Marie's knack for taking whatever life dealt her with a smile. After the dentist told her she needed several fillings, she gushed to me about how much she liked the strawberry-flavored fluoride.

Eventually, I realized that Marie didn't see me as the adult who would fix her life. Marie didn't see anything wrong with her life.

She was good, however, at helping me see what was wrong

with mine. One time, she suggested swimming as our weekly activity. I was so self-conscious about my body that I hadn't been to a pool in nearly ten years. She quickly let me know how silly I was. Swimming was fun, and I was missing out on a lot by not going, she said. Who cares what everyone else thinks?

I couldn't say no to that grin of hers, so I suited up. But I kept my shorts over my bathing suit and draped a towel over me, as well. Marie confidently ran for the water in her two-piece bathing suit, while I kept dry and covered up. When I finally stripped down to my swimsuit, my cheeks burned with embarrassment at my shape. As soon as I slid into the pool, Marie challenged me to a swimming contest. Before long, I forgot to worry about what the dozens of other swimmers around me might think about my overweight body. Swimming became a regular event for us.

Marie helped me see how my low self-esteem had become an inhibitor in other aspects of my life. Shyness had kept me from trying new things. Like many self-conscious people, I'd assumed that others would be riveted by any awkwardness I displayed, and that such attention would be unbearable. Marie challenged me on this shyness almost every week—like the time she insisted we go to the local art museum and spend a few hours drawing our favorite paintings. I was worried sick that people would laugh at my work. Marie, on the other hand, stopped dozens of passersby for their opinions of her drawings. She had no qualms about engaging strangers in conversation, and I saw I didn't have to be nearly as fearful as I was.

It has been nearly two years since Marie and I became "siblings." Although I sometimes still complain about my life, I do it much less now because I know Marie wouldn't tolerate my negativity. And while the idea of meeting new people still gives me pause, I usually get over being scared by invoking Marie's outgoing example.

I'd been right that holiday season when I decided that something was missing in my life. I was wrong, however, to think my happiness would be found in being someone's savior. What was really missing was a selfless two-way friendship. Maybe such a friendship is charity in the truest sense of the word. The outings I've been able to offer Marie may have marginally brightened her life, but her impact on mine has been huge.

These days I would never call Marie a charity case. Now I just call her sister.

Becky Mollenkamp is Features and Travel Editor for Better Homes and Gardens.

LOVE'S LABOR FOUND

Robert Tucker

The story I'm about to tell concerns a young man who lives in a New England suburb and an elderly woman who was a close friend of mine. I'm going to call the fellow Jake— and I'm going to disguise some other details here, too.

The ground for Jake's deed was seeded when he was a small boy, growing up in a household where both his mom and dad worked full-time. Jake and his baby brother were left in the charge of a fine woman named Serene Boise. By the time she came to help out Jake's family, she had already raised her own brood and cared for some of her grandchildren, too.

Serene Boise didn't have much in the way of goods, but she had a large spirit that infected Jake in the best possible way. She took his childish concerns seriously, hugging him when it thundered, ferreting out his worry the time it snowed in October. He was upset, it turned out, because the birds had no winter coats. His father laughed when he came home and Mrs. Boise repeated that. But Serene thought it showed that, young as the boy was, he had a Christian spirit.

Serene was a religious woman. As Jake and his brother got older, she told them many stories of people who were able to endure hardship because they had strong faith. Jake's parents were the kind who thought that while inspirational stories were all very well for children, the business of adults was, well, business. It grieved Mrs. Boise that Jake and his brother were not sent to Sunday school.

It disturbed Jake's parents, I suspect, that Mrs. Boise's eggs were all in the Jesus basket. The year winter came so early, Mrs. Boise's old furnace died and she had no money to replace it. She didn't like to mention this to her employers, although it was cer-

tainly terrible for her and those in her family—a disabled husband and a divorced daughter with four kids of her own—who
remained in the house. But Jake's mother learned of it one afternoon when she drove Mrs. Boise home. After she and her husband gave Mrs. Boise the money for a down payment on a new
furnace, Serene exclaimed, "I prayed and Jesus heard me." I
guessed that Jake's father and mother would have preferred
being thanked more directly.

Mrs. Boise remained Jake's baby-sitter until his family moved
to somewhere near Baltimore. When they came back up north it
was to another state, and by then Jake didn't need babysitting.
He remained in touch with Serene, sending her cards and occasionally telephoning.

Suddenly, Serene's health went. It took her a few weeks to get
around to a doctor, and then there were more doctors, and what
she heard was that she had a cancer too far-gone for treatment.
Serene Boise accepted this. When you look at death as coming
home, it doesn't seem so bad. Her main concern was that she'd
be able to say good-bye to everyone in her far-flung family.

In June, Jake came to visit on his way to his summer job as a
counselor at a sleep-away camp. He was sixteen or seventeen
and very excited about the job. Serene told him her doctor did-
n't think she'd last the summer, but that she fully intended, with
the Lord's help, to celebrate one more Christmas.

It was Jake who broke the sad news to his parents, in a call he
made from the village outside the camp. They telephoned Serene,
and sent up a big Fourth-of-July picnic basket, which was very
nice for Mrs. Boise's daughter and their neighbors. Serene
enjoyed the day tremendously, although she couldn't eat from
the basket.

After Jake had been at the camp awhile, he told his parents
he'd taken on the extra job of cleaning latrines—for a $500

bonus. "What do you need the money for?" they asked. But he wouldn't tell.

Jake's father guessed that Jake wanted it for a secondhand motorbike, because that was what he, himself, secretly had bought when he went away to college. But he no more approved the idea than his own father had, which is why he thought Jake was remaining mum.

Jake's mother was plagued with worry. Why did her son so badly need cash? Surely, scrubbing the camp outhouses was an awful job. For one thing, Jake had to get up at 5 a.m. to do it, and Jake was a boy who liked his sleep. She'd heard that maybe two dozen boys used each facility, and that by night they depended on flashlights. A boys' camp latrine had to be an unholy mess.

The truth came out in a frantic phone call that Jake made in August. He told his folks that the $500 was to buy Mrs. Boise a round-trip air ticket to Seattle so she could visit her married son and grandchildren there in September. But he had to get the ticket right away or the price would go higher. He didn't have the cash in hand, and he'd realized that even if he could raise it there was no travel agent in the town near the camp. He asked his parents to please purchase the ticket on his behalf—and he'd pay them back.

After Jake's parents got over their amazement (and yes, relief), second thoughts took hold. Serene Boise was a very sick woman; wouldn't it be better for her son to come to her? He already had, Jake explained. But Mrs. Boise wanted to say good-bye to her daughter-in-law and her five grandchildren in Seattle, too—no way could they afford six tickets. Besides, Mrs. Boise wanted to see the Pacific Ocean before she died—she'd told him that, years ago.

But in a month, Mrs. Boise might be unable to travel, she

might not even be . . . around. "Mrs. Boise is going to live until after Christmas," Jake said definitely. But she can't make this trip alone, they said. Jake, finally exasperated, said he knew that. Her daughter was going with her.

Jake stayed at the camp a week after it closed to help shut it down for the season. He got $150 for that, which he figured Mrs. Boise could use. Serene and her daughter flew to Seattle the next month. The older woman was in a wheelchair and probably in considerable pain, which she ignored. When they returned, Serene Boise said the visit had been wonderful.

December was a hard month for Serene who remained at home. But on Christmas Eve she refused her painkillers, her daughter said, so she could be alert to celebrate baby Jesus and not be confused in her prayers.

Jake, his younger brother and their parents attended Serene's funeral, which took place in January. In the afternoon, some folks gathered at our house and talked about Serene. Jake's mother told me about the latrine cleaning while she was helping in the kitchen. She added it wasn't something he bragged on or liked to mention, which is why I've changed his name here.

It started to snow toward evening, and I recalled the story of the birds without winter coats, but I didn't repeat it then.

Robert Tucker lives in Maine.

CHARITY UNDER FIRE
Rob Schultheis

I t was the winter of 1984; Afghanistan, my first war. Things were going badly for the *mujahedin*, the so-called "holy warriors" of the anti-Soviet resistance. In the Safed Koh Mountains, where I was reporting for *Time*, the skies were literally filled with Russian-built jets and helicopter gun-ships, bombing, rocketing, firing cannons and machineguns.

Most of the local villages were deserted, bombed into rubble, their orchards shattered by rockets and their fields sown with deadly anti-personnel mines. Every few days, a phalanx of airborne commandos would land, burn a few of the remaining houses and kill anyone they caught.

In the midst of this hellscape, my Afghan translator Etibari and I headed back toward the Pakistani border from the frontlines south of Kabul. It was bitter cold, and snow was falling. Toward dusk, in a barren little badlands valley, we came upon a small village that had somehow survived the bombardments: a cluster of adobe-walled houses against a hillside, fallow snow-covered fields, crude corrals of sheep and goats.

Etibari wanted to keep going. He wasn't sure if the villagers were friendly, or if they had gone over to the Russian side in order to survive. But one of the villagers, an ancient goatherd clothed in rags, with a snow-white Santa Claus beard, spotted us and came running, shouting, beckoning for us to come with him. He led us up through the village, through a set of big, carved wooden gates, through a muddy courtyard into his house. We were his guests, he told us with a benign smile. It was an honor to have us visit his poor village. "No traveler is a stranger in Afghanistan," he said, quoting an old Pushtun saying.

That night, we sat by a roaring woodstove, eating a feast fit for kings: Thick, rich goat yogurt. Slabs of warm wheat bread. Chunks of juicy lamb. Cornbread. Raisins and nuts. Cup after cup of strong green tea, spiked with sugar. As we ate, our host beamed and beamed at us. Other villagers—elders, young farmers, kids clad in butterfly-bright colors—peered at us through the door and windows. Outside, the wind howled, the snows flew. But we sat in the warmest room in the world, surrounded by strangers who were suddenly our dearest friends.

The next morning the storm had broken, and we prepared to leave. Etibari took me aside, out of earshot of our host. He had been asking and looking around the village, and discovered that our host and his fellow-villagers were nearly starving to death. Many of the young men had gone away to fight the Russians and never returned. The sheep and goatherds had been machine-gunned from the air, and many animals had been lost. The man we had stayed with, who was the caretaker of the village mosque, was the poorest man in the village. He had spent every coin he had, and then some, and had emptied his larder to serve us, his honored guests, that fabulous dinner.

"What should we do?" I asked.

"We can't give him money," said Etibari. "The shame of it would kill him." I looked across the courtyard, to where our host was talking with the other villagers, trying to find out the safest route for us to take to the border. He caught my eye and smiled, tilting his head gently in that old Asian gesture that conveys a whole universe of unspoken sympathy, empathy.

I made an effort to keep my voice steady and my eyes dry. "What if we offer a contribution to the village mosque?" I suggested. "Isn't that traditional? You can tell him I'm a foreign Moslem, and I want to help my fellows with their place of faith. Hell, you can tell him it's an American Moslem tradition if you want."

Etibari grinned at me. "You know, Rob, you'd make a good

Afghan," he whispered.

I took almost all the money in my pocket, a damp roll of Afghani bank notes and Pakistani rupees, and slipped it to Etibari. He produced an envelope from his pack, put the money in it, and we went over to our host. Etibari spoke to him, and then took the old man's hands in his and pressed the envelope between them. The wrinkled old mountain shepherd looked us both in the eyes. Tears began to run down his face as he smiled at us, the biggest smile I had seen yet. He hugged Etibari. Then he hugged me, hugged me till I thought my ribs were going to crack.

As we walked away from the village, following the trail south into the hills, I looked back and saw him waving to us. Five minutes later I looked back again: He was still there. Just as the trail turned up around the curve of the first hill, I looked back one last time. The old man was still waving, and, though he was a tiny speck, I swear I could still see him smiling.

Three years later, I came that way again. But this time the village was gone: nothing but burnt rubble on the mountainside. A cluster of graves stood off to one side, covered with the green funeral banners of Islam that say: Here lie the faithful, slain fighting for God.

We asked a couple of herdsmen nearby what had happened. The Russians heard the people here were sheltering the *muja-hedin* and their friends, they told us. One day they landed here in helicopters, many soldiers. They rounded up the villagers and killed them all. Then they burned the village to the ground.

Rob Schultheis continues to report on human rights in Afghanistan. His most recent book, Fool's Gold *(Lyons Press, 2001), is about life in the Rockies.*

CLEMENCY

Tekla Dennison Miller

J amie spent her first fifteen months of life in prison. She was one of the lucky ones. She was a reject and got out early.

Jamie is my golden retriever. Her full name is Jamie Newbarker. The inmates named her after James Neubaucher, a journalist who wrote about the disabled for the *Detroit Free Press*. Jamie was one of the puppies trained in the late 1980s by women prisoners as leader dogs for Michigan's Rochester School for the Blind. At that time, I was the warden for the Huron Valley Women's Facility.

The puppy training for prisoners began when Carol Dyer, a reading teacher, and Janelle, a prisoner, approached me with a well-thought-out proposal to implement a vocational program. My first reaction was, "The central office administration will never go for it."

Janelle looked at me with beseeching eyes and said, "Oh pleeeze, Warden Miller, try to persuade them."

I love dogs and was aware of the research showing the benefits their presence brought to any institution, including fewer fights. Yet I wasn't sure the director and the corrections commissioners were ready for this leap. The only program like it in the United States was at the Women's Prison in Tacoma, Washington.

A week later Carol and I presented our plans to the five-member commission and the director of corrections. They leafed through our written proposal and listened with what appeared to be half-hearted attention. Disappointed in their apparent lack of interest, I finished my lecture, statistics and all, saying, "It's a cost-effective way to have a productive and marketable vocational program for the inmates." On an impulse I added, "It will also teach the prisoners to give back to the community."

I had expected the commissioners and director would give us their usual exit speech, "Thank you for coming today, Warden Miller. We'll get back with you within the month."

Instead, Chairman Waters said, "We love this program. How soon can you get started?"

Carol's mouth dropped open and I fumbled with the papers I was trying to stuff into my attaché. "Umm," I said, "right away."

When Carol and I were in the hall outside the conference room, I turned to her and asked, "Now what?"

"We have a lot of work to do," she said with confidence, and headed for the door.

Within six months, kennels were built, prisoners were recruited, the local kennel club was alerted and the Leader Dog School sent puppies. Veterinary services, dog food and other supplies were donated by the Rochester School, making it cost-effective and appealing to the state's budget and management accountants.

Before the dogs arrived, Carol gave classes for the prisoners about the program itself. And she taught them general commands. Even so, when the first puppies came, the women weren't totally prepared for how to handle the live animals. On the first day of actual training, the enthusiastic puppies dragged the prisoners across the training quad. But with the help of trainers from local kennel clubs, who worked with the prisoners, within a month the inmate trainers start-

"It is another's fault if he be ungrateful, but it is mine if I do not give. To find one thankful man, I will oblige a great many that are not so."—Seneca

ed to look like they were in control. The puppies heeled and stayed when told.

In the second month, Janelle, the inmate who had pleaded for the program and who was Jamie's trainer, said to me, "You know, Warden Miller, working with these dogs is like being a good mother."

"I hadn't really thought about that," I said, "but you are absolutely right."

Together we listed some of the traits the women were learning: unconditional love, tolerance, discipline, anger control, cleaning up, good grooming, nutrition, trust and patience. The dogs were with the prisoners almost every moment of the day, placed in their kennels only at night.

After our list making, Janelle returned to her training duties. Watching her maneuver Jamie toward Officer Bates, a veteran guard not known for his compassion, I wondered what their meeting would provoke. I was surprised to see Bates lean down to pet Jamie, and I eavesdropped as he and Janelle started talking about the dogs' training, and Jamie's recent diagnosis of hip dysplasia.

I smiled. The dogs were not only helping the prisoners, they were helping prisoner-guard relationships, too. Officers and inmates now had a common subject about which they could talk without being defensive.

Though the dogs didn't officially graduate until after another four weeks of residential training at the Rochester school, we had a pre-graduation ceremony for our part of the training. We invited the dog owners, the press and the commissioners. Janelle spoke for the inmates: "Before I came to the Valley, I was a prostitute and a drug addict," she said. "I never finished high school and I was pregnant at fourteen." Mascara-streaked tears began to stream down her face. She blew her nose before going on. "Today, I believe I can conquer anything because, for the first time in my life, I am able to give back to society."

She was using the words I had said to the director and commissioners when I was trying to sell them the puppy training idea. The director eyed me with suspicion, as if I had prepared Janelle's speech.

While Janelle paused to catch her breath, the room was so quiet. The only sound came from the panting dogs. "I never thought anyone believed I was worthy enough to give back to my community. And I thank everyone in this room for that."

There wasn't a dry eye among the assembled audience, not even that of the reporter, James Neubaucher. Jamie lay at his feet. She didn't graduate because of the hip dysplasia. The infirmity would eventually make her arthritic, rendering her in need of more help than a blind partner could provide.

Jamie's rejection wasn't taken lightly by the women in the program. They saw Jamie's failure as their own. I was afraid they might fall back into their negative behavior patterns of blaming someone for what had happened to Jamie, of refusing to face up to the situation or denying it was real. Instead, after the pre-graduation ceremonies and a few days of brooding, they came up with a proposal, which they presented to the director of the Leader Dog School for the Blind. They asked the Rochester School administration to use Jamie's picture on the graduation certificate given out at the end of the four-week residential training. They also began sewing scarves to be worn by their puppies still in training, which said "Future Leader Dog."

The inmates' final gracious act was to convince the director of the Leader Dog School to give me Jamie. I've been the direct beneficiary of the inmates' training, because Jamie has been a loving and loyal companion to my husband and me ever since.

Although the inmates were the ones who did most of the giv-

> *"The sage does not accumulate for himself. The more he uses for others, the more he has himself. The more he gives to others, the more he possesses of his own."*—Lao-tzu

ing—from the training to making me a present of Jamie herself, in the end they were the ones who received. As one prisoner wrote to me: "This program has given me a purpose in life and helped me to realize that I do have self-worth and can help others. Had it not been for my involvement in this program, I would still be using drugs and not caring about anyone or anything, least of all myself. Being able to see the joy in the faces of the people that receive our service dogs has given me a reason to continue on with life."

Tekla Dennison Miller, author of The Warden Wore Pink *(Biddle Publishing), is the former warden of two maximum-security prisons. She is now a criminal justice consultant in Durango, Colorado.*

THE OLD HORSES

John Nelson

Sometimes, I get a restless feeling,
a yearning hard to explain,
a need to soothe an uneasy soul,
to let spirits soar again.

Then I go out among the horses
just to watch them move,
to know the peaceful fluid wander,
the rise and fall of hoove.

I go there just to be alone, yet
not to be alone at all.
Their nicker warms a place inside.
My spirit heeds their call.

I know each one by a given name,
and they all know me.
Some are just like old close friends.
Some don't care to be.

For some, we've partnered twenty years,
others a year or two.
Some bring back cherished memories
of the things we used to do.

And, I worry about these old ones
whose usefulness has passed.
Oh, they were proud. They earned their keep.
But good times just don't last.

How can I afford to support them
at the price of land and feed?
With swayed backs and rheumy eyes,
they've lived beyond their need.

There's those who'd say I'm foolish
for keeping horses past their prime.
That you can't run a charity and
do business the same time.

They say there's no value in mounts
that do not earn their hay.
That money spent on boarding them
is money thrown away.

But value isn't always measured
by the amount of work that's done.
And sometimes on cold mornings
when the old ones buck and run

it brings back the spunk and spirit
of the early days we rode,
renews my smile, and that makes them
worth more to me than gold.

Cowboy poet John Nelson, author of My Participle's Danglin', *owns
the Gunnison Country Guide Service, which runs horse and mule
pack trips into the Colorado wilderness and the Utah canyon country.*

THE NECKLACE
Janice H. Mikesell

L et me tell you about a special afternoon. In the car: my brother, myself, my four children, still very small. My husband wasn't with us; he was visiting his parents. We drove through St. Louis, deeper and deeper into the terrible downtown. Knowing every street, every building, every memory—sad that I ever had to leave, still sad after all these years. Pulling into the Corcoran Gardens, no gardens at all, only cement. Seeing the sweet face at the window, five floors up, head tilted, hand waving. Our eyes met; everyone waved in unison.

We found a parking place where the car could easily be checked from the window. Locked up tight. All of us were in our best clothes, bearing presents. Through the dark entry, up the rickety elevator, down the urine-soaked, graffiti-streaked halls, knocking on the heavy door. Various locks unclicking, the door finally opening. The smiling face having rejoined the body—so old, so stooped and frail. If I were to sit on her lap now, her bones would turn to powder.

"Come in, come in," Gausie said, in the voice I remembered. She sat us down. The children were even bigger than last year, she said. I was the same, and my brother was a welcome sight after all these years. She set our gifts aside for later. For now, we must give an accounting of ourselves.

As the others talked, I looked around. The apartment was clean except for the dingy priscilla curtains parted limply over the windows. How I wished I could take them home, wash them, starch them, iron them and put them back up. But I knew I couldn't dare ask. Each windowsill between the parted curtains was set with potted plants, the kind of pots that were wrapped in silver foil colored on the inside—the kind of plants that had hairy leaves and teensy-tiny flowers. I saw the curio shelves that held a collection of miniature ceramic horses. And on a corner table, an artificial Christmas tree was hung with silver icicles, the base wrapped in cotton batting covered with little sparkles. Our gifts were placed there, keeping company with a couple of others. The upholstered furniture was massive and old, with high backs and arms bordered with carved polished wood. It was all rather grand and probably inherited from her deceased sister.

You see, that was the way of the Irish, she had told me. They took each other in. When she had been widowed, "her people," as she called them, had taken her in. Since she had also lost her own little girl, she had been perfect for raising her relatives' children. First she had raised the Gause girls, then the Bulfin boy and girl, and then, when she finally ran out of relatives' children to raise, she had raised me. My parents had hired her to raise their very lively little girl, and she had lived with us for the first twelve years of my life.

"There is no one to stand up for this little girl," she had said. "I will stand up for her." And even when my brother had been born, those words had held true. "You are my little girl," she had said—and that was that.

She set the Formica table with heavy plates, everyday flatwear and tall, ice-filled glasses. She brought out a chocolate-frosted cake and a half-gallon of vanilla ice cream. She cut the cake, which was yellow inside, into huge slabs and topped them with mounds of ice cream. She filled each glass from a liter bottle of Coca Cola. "Eat up," she said, smiling. "There's plenty more." We knew our duty, had seconds, declined thirds.

This is what civilization is about, I thought. All those millions of years: out of the water, out of the slime, up on two legs, forming clans, forming cities, forming cultures. It all leads to this little room with its dingy curtains and dry yellow cake with everyone taking seconds and being nice to each other. This is the stopping place.

She told us about the events of the past year. This was a strangely happy time for her. Although she regretted the passing of an ill sister (of whom she had been taking care), Gausie, at age ninety-three, was finally liberated from most chores. A social worker, who was also a nun, came to visit twice a week, and that was very nice. Someone from the church picked her up for Sunday mass and special devotions. And the Maschmeyers, who were "her people" once removed, took her home for Sunday dinner, also assisting with groceries and laundry. Best of all, Frank, the Bulfin boy, so damaged from the war, was given furlough from the psychiatric hospital twice each year to come and stay with her. Frank was the reason she was at Corcoran Gardens instead of Catholic Charities, which my mother could have easily gotten her into. Catholic Charities didn't have an extra room for Frank.

We gave her our gifts and she appreciated them. We sang "Silent Night," she in the sweet, fragile voice I'd always loved. She left the room briefly and returned with a small gift. "I'm sorry I don't have presents for the others," she said, "but it's so hard for me to get out and shop."

There was a folded note inside the box. It was dated 1937. "Dear Gausie," it said, "I found these beads in Rome, and I thought you might enjoy them. Sincerely, Julane Davis."

The necklace had been a gift to her from my own Aunt Julia, another champion of my childhood. My glamorous Aunt Julia from California, practically a movie star, having worked as a

> *"The manner of giving is worth more than the gift."*
> —Pierre Corneille

stand-in for Jeanette McDonald and Ann Harding. My Aunt Julia, who always eyed my older sisters suspiciously and told my mother that I was the artistic one, just like her. I lifted the multi-colored glass beads from their box. It was too much. My brother saw me turn away, ashamed of my tears.

"She saved this necklace for me for all these years," I told my mother later on.

"They're just cheap colored glass," my mother countered, quick as a slap. "They're not worth anything."

I was stunned.

"There is no one to stand up for that little girl," Gausie had said. "I will stand up for her." These are the words that rang out from my childhood. These words were the best gift of all.

Janice H. Mikesell is the author of six chapbooks ranging from poetry to satire to nostalgia to a children's book. She is a PEN Syndicated Fiction Project winner and has been awarded a South Dakota Arts Council Fellowship in literature.

SECTION II

♦CHARITY BEGINS AT HOME♦

"A Helping Hand", Renouf, 1881, Perry Pictures

"Oh lady! We receive but what we give."

—SAMUEL TAYLOR COLERIDGE

MY EX-FATHER-IN-LAW
Daniel Asa Rose

J ust because you break up with a woman is no reason to break up with her dad. You still use the squash racquet he gave you one Christmas, after all. You still haven't quite gotten around to tossing out the bay rum aftershave he gave you during Reagan's first term. In my case, it's the front lawn that keeps me connected. Every time I mow the lawn, I remember when he drove cross-country to visit and parked his Porsche defiantly center-grass, where he felt a driveway should be, rather than behind the house, where I had one paved. How can you break up with the people in your past, even when they happen to be your basic ex-father-in-law from hell?

For in actual truth, Wesley and I had never gotten along. I took my cue from the father-daughter axis that was already in place when I got there. He bullied her, she cried; she baited him, he bit. They were perfect for each other. When I married Laura, they courteously widened the dynamic to include me. Before long, I too was baiting and biting to beat the band, taking Laura's side to Wesley, taking the old man's side to my wife. Brandy in hand, I would stay up till two in the morning in the kitchen with Wes, trying to explicate his daughter to him, while he reduced sauces and took pot shots at alleged lapses in my grammar; then I'd mount the stairs and get side-blasted by my wife for cozying up to the enemy. Bridegrooms take note: This is a thankless position to be in.

But what a worthy enemy he was. Just to call him a retired physicist who cooked gourmet is not to do justice to the full cantankerous hulk of the man. Barrel-chested and bullheaded, with enough piss 'n' vinegar to insure that he would live to be one hundred, he was also a robust and unrepentant womanizer, a bomber pilot who had once flown thirty-five missions over Germany, a man who'd been gypped out of his credit for electrifying the organ, and a gifted oil painter on the side. A self-portrait he did in his youth shows a dashing spirit: wind-blown, courageous, and something else—mean. The man definitely had a mean streak. He looked and acted a lot like Gene Hackman in *Unforgiven*: genial-sadistic, with a snare-drum laugh that did not mind if it caused pain.

Laura, herself, was a match for her pop—glamorous and tough. Their fights were legion. Into this maelstrom I gallantly marched, dancing the 2 a.m. fool's dance of defending each to the other. Soon, neither would talk to me. Inevitably, all the bitterness Wes had amassed against his daughter was aimed in my direction. And Laura started treating me as she had always treated her father: rebelling, even, as though it were I who had grounded her for her entire senior year, I who had ripped off my dinner jacket and chased her hippie friends from her debutante ball with a butcher knife.

And so, seven years after making both their rather colorful acquaintances, I courteously narrowed the dynamic by accepting my wife's divorce. They were left to themselves. It became no longer his business how many modifiers were allegedly left dangling. Contact with the father-in-law was lapsed.

Five years passed.

And then, having returned from a trip to Tibet, I was given to understand that Wes had been hospitalized. I was startled to find old-fashioned "endearments" spring to my mind: why the old warhorse, the old coot, the old codger, had been laid low at last. Everything was starting to go: his liver backed-up, his hemorrhoids burned, his toes turned black.

Though we hadn't spoken in five years, I sent him a batch of prayer beads I'd bartered for in Shigatse. "These are from the

TWO SIDES OF THE MOON

In Nigeria, the Ekoi have a double-edged legend of the moon. An antelope and sheep are farmers. A hungry crocodile asks for food from the antelope, who is deaf to his request. The generous sheep, however, offers plantains. The crocodile returns to the river and shares the sheep's gift with the python. The thankful python takes from his head a shining stone and gives it to the crocodile to show the sheep. The stone is so brilliant that it lights the darkness as the crocodile makes his way back to the sheep's farm. The sheep is so thrilled by the glowing rock he trades his farm for it, and displays his stone outdoors so all might share its beauty.

But without the farm, the sheep finds himself starving. He approaches his former neighbor, but the miserly antelope refuses to give him dinner. Other farmer-animals also refuse to share their crops, telling the sheep he was a fool to swap his means of living for a stone that illuminates the dark.

Weak and weary, the sheep staggers on until he happens upon the god, Effion Obassi, who is harvesting palm kernels. Effion Obassi shares these kernels with the newcomer. The grateful sheep offers his one treasure to the god, who accepts it and takes it to the sky people.

These sky lords place the luminous stone in a box. To remind humans of the sheep's generosity, they open the box each month, and the moon's light shines on earth to benefit all. But the gods also close the box so that we may take heed of the darkness of selfishness.

Dalai Lama to heal you back to health," I wrote. "The kids need a grandpa who keeps on ticking."

He rallied. He was home from the hospital, in his silk robe, chasing the private nurse. He was well enough to take up the pen in his crabbed hand. Four months after I sent him the beads an envelope arrived: just my name and my town, no street, no zip code—definitive proof that the bullheadedness was intact. Unsealing the letter, I had to wonder why I was letting him park on my front lawn again. For here was the bitterness spewing forth unabated, as though the faucet had been stopped up these five years and now flooded forth to catalogue all my generation's ancient arrogance, our impertinence, our lack of respect for our elders. He also enclosed a copy of *Strunk and White*, in case my grammar was still remiss, ha ha. But then the tone softened. He was talking about something new. About why our youthful arrogance had irked him, about how he himself had once had a hard time coming to grips with his place in the world and learning to respect his elders. The tone was better than fatherly: it was a sharing as equals. It ended with these incredible words: "Can we not forgive each other our faults?"

After a month, I at last discovered what to send him back. I packed up a tape of Siobhan McKenna singing various passages from *Finnegan's Wake*. "It may not be grammatical," I said, "but can we agree it's music?"

I told him I regretted wasting those 2 a.m.s sparring instead of learning his technique for reducing sauces. I asked him if he was planning to fly any more bombing missions over Germany. I spoke of how well my sons, his grandchildren, were doing, and said I saluted him across the gene pool. "Here, here," I said, metaphorically raising one of the brandy glasses we used to share, "let's do forgive and celebrate. I toast your renewable good health."

So it's easy, is it not? To pick up where you left off. There is no earthly reason to stop communicating with a man just because you divorced his daughter, no reason in the world not to keep the dialogue going ad infinitum. Except one. For this bullying bruiser who was going to live to be one hundred suddenly dropped, just like that. Before I could send off my package, this unstoppable man with his burly chest and nasty brilliance was cut down, the private nurse un-caught, the hurtful snare drum of a laugh shut down at last.

I had meant to pick up where we left off: Now we were just leaving off. Wesley Love died, and what was music and what was not would have to wait for some later debate.

Here's to you, ex-father-in-law. I'm sorry we never recognized each other for what we were. Probably you were not the ogre I thought, just a mortal straining to suck in your gut in your canary yellow La Coste shirt. I was just a kid trying to lock horns with one of the big guys. Why didn't we know that then? Why aren't we all more gentle with each other now?

Daniel Asa Rose is an O. Henry Prize-winning short story writer. His latest book is HIDING PLACES: a Father and His Sons Retrace Their Family's Escape From the Holocaust *(Simon & Schuster). He lives in Massachusetts*

And throughout all eternity,
I forgive you, you forgive me.
—William Blake

THE DAUGHTER'S NEW CLOTHES
Rosemerry Wahtola Trommer

Dark blue velvet, the dress you stitched for me,
with a white eyelet bib and a rounded lace collar.

I wore it once for midnight Christmas mass, kneeling
between you and Dad, holding a thin white candle in a cup.

That night, I felt like a gift, something treasured and worthy,
wrapped with intention and offered with love to the world.

I grew out of the dress two months after you made it,
the shoulders too tight, the new plastic zipper reluctant.

As my sleeve lengths stretched out and inseams matured,
you knit me a coat of prayers I couldn't grow out of, only grow into.

And wearing it now with its cuffs just right, I feel like a present,
wrapped with warm intention and offered with love to the world.

A LONG WAR ENDS

William Noble

My Norwegian-American wife was fifty years old before she set foot in the land her parents had emigrated from. It wasn't until the early 1970s, after both of June's parents had passed on, that we visited Norway.

World War II had thrust a king-sized wedge into her family. The argument was over political sympathy with Hitler and Nazi Germany. Before the war, a Norwegian National Socialist (Nazi) Party had emerged, headed by Vidkun Quisling (whose name was to become synonymous with "treason"). While Quisling's party never achieved more than five percent of the popular vote in any election during the 1930s, the allure of connection to Nazi Germany had attracted followers, including members of my wife's family.

History has recorded what happened in Norway on April 8, 1940. Without warning, German troops invaded by land and sea, Norway's major cities were bombed, and the Norwegian government fled north. At 7 p.m. that same evening, Vidkun Quisling went on Norwegian state radio and declared himself "Minister-President" of Norway. "All resistance is futile," he announced. "Lay down your arms!" And, with the backing of German troops, he and his followers took over the country.

At this time, my wife and her immediate family were safe and secure in America. But most other members of the family who had remained in Norway had to suffer through five years of German occupation. Some of her relatives, however, thrived: Esther, her father's favorite sister, and Olaf and Ivar, two of Esther's sons. They embraced the Quisling philosophy of collaboration with the Nazis and lived well until the war was over.

Afterward, of course, came the accounting. Quisling was tried for war crimes and executed in October 1945. Esther and her family were stripped of most material possessions, and Olaf and Ivar went to prison. The rest of the family treated Esther, Olaf and Ivar as if they had died. No one would have anything to do with them.

As the 1940s became the 1950s and then the 1960s, my wife corresponded with and entertained other members of her Norwegian family when they came to the United States, but no one spoke of Esther, Olaf or Ivar. All my wife knew was snippets from their lives before 1945. Esther had married well and had been a close friend of explorer Roald Amundsen, the first human to reach the South Pole. Esther had even baked special cakes for Amundsen to carry on his 1910-1911 expedition. Olaf had been a talented writer and journalist and had worked for *Dagbladet*, the largest Norwegian daily newspaper. He had been a correspondent in Vienna and Paris during the 1930s. Before the war, Ivar had been a small businessman, running an electrical repair shop but giving support to Norwegian National Socialism and Quisling's policies.

It disturbed my wife that a single branch of the family remained outcasts, even though they lived thousands of miles away and their beliefs were so different from hers. June had grown up as a patriotic American. Her parents were American citizens and her brother had been a U.S. Army major and a member of the OSS, with responsibility for Norwegian resistance liaison.

After we decided to visit Norway in 1971, my wife planned our itinerary with a view to seeing as many relatives as possible. Still, the names Esther, Olaf and Ivar did not pass her lips. But that didn't mean she hadn't been thinking of them. As we flew across the Atlantic, she showed me a calendar—each day corresponded to the name of a relative and the town, village or city in

Norway where we would be.

I noticed two days in Oslo were left blank, and I pointed this out.

"I'm not sure . . . " she began. Then she took a deep breath. "I want to contact Esther's family."

"Suppose they don't want to see you?"

She was silent a moment. "My father would want me to do this." Her father had left the legacy of his closeness to Esther, and my wife must have felt that in the bones of her being.

In a few days we arrived in Oslo, and I could see my wife working on what she would say.

"Are you sure this is wise?" I asked one more time. "Maybe you'll open old wounds."

My wife shook her head. "My father would want this, and I know it's right."

So she placed a call to Olaf, who was about her age. She identified herself in Norwegian as her father's daughter and said she was in Oslo. There must have been shocked silence on the other end of the phone. "Are you there?" she resumed in a kind voice. Then, "No, this is not a joke."

Tears welled in her eyes; her voice grew shaky. "Yes," she said, "I'm here with my husband. We want to see you."

More silence. "That happened a long time ago," she said.

We agreed to meet Olaf in the lobby of a downtown Oslo hotel later that day and, as we sat awaiting Olaf, my wife said to me, "I have no idea what he looks like, but I know I'll recognize him."

Sure enough, a few moments later, she uttered a little cry, jumped to her feet and threw her arms about a tall, gaunt man who was approaching. Then, she brought him over to me, stroking his shoulder and neck. "My cousin," she said softly, "my cousin."

In the next two days we met both Ivar and Esther, the mother.

"My father would approve," my wife kept repeating. "He would approve."

Esther, who by this time was in her mid-eighties, had recently suffered a stroke. Her mind was clear though her speech was slurred. Yet when she saw my wife, she whispered, "My brother's baby!" and tears streamed down her face. My wife went over to her, they hugged and whispered to one another, and it was clear that whatever demons the past had created were now put to rest.

We had a final cup of coffee with Olaf before boarding the train to take us to see yet another relative. Somberly, he presented my wife with a bound notebook. "I have kept this all these years," he said. "I want you to have it." On his face was a mixture of pride and pain. "Please!"

It was the daily journal he had kept in prison, his reflections, his recounting of events, his growing religious faith. "It's how I found God," he said, "and you have made it all come true." He reached out to my wife and squeezed her hand. "Thank you," he whispered.

William Noble has written sixteen books, most recently Writing Dramatic Nonfiction, *which was a selection of the Writer's Digest Book Club. He also has co-authored five books with his wife. He lives in New Jersey, where he teaches creative writing.*

THE LIST

Beth Lynn Clegg

"**A**re you asleep?" Ann asked as she shook her husband's shoulder. When Les responded with indistinguishable sounds, a more vigorous shake followed. "Wake up. I want to talk to you. I've compiled a list of our friends, any of who will be a good wife for you when I'm dead. Are you awake?"

"I am now."

Ann and Les had been in Japan when an infection had settled in Ann's eyes, seriously impairing her vision. They traveled with their newborn son back to the States for medical treatment. Thus began a search that continued for the rest of Ann's life. Despite examinations by the foremost authorities in ophthalmology and write-ups in medical journals worldwide, the source of Ann's infection was never detected. Eventually, the mysterious infection dismantled her immune system, and cancer took hold. Despite decades of medical problems, Ann remained cheerful. With the end in sight, she remained upbeat and pragmatic.

Ann had been my friend since first grade, and our roads kept intersecting and reconnecting for over sixty years. There were periods when we didn't have contact for five to ten years, yet, when we hooked up again, it was always as if we merely hadn't chatted for a few days. The last time we reconnected we were both in our mid-sixties, and I'd just moved to Houston, where Ann and Les were living.

Ann confided in me how she fretted over the increasing demands her health problems made on Les. But he took the grocery shopping, meal preparations and medical assistance in stride. He was devoted to Ann and enjoyed the opportunity to care for her. Ann's friends saw the immensity of Les' generosity, and it endeared Les to us even more.

A carrot salad, which Les seemed to enjoy, was my contribution to an impromptu December lunch with both of them shortly after I'd settled back in Houston. It was during that lunch I first heard of "the list."

While we were eating, Ann told me how one sleepless night she'd evaluated each of six friends she believed would be a suitable companion for her beloved husband after she'd passed away. The next morning she had articulated their strengths and weaknesses to Les. Believing the facts presented to be irrefutable, she repeated them to me. I eyed Les for his response.

Tongue in cheek, he replied, "That's a great list, but I have one of my own."

Laughter is, indeed, good for the digestion.

However, when Ann suggested I should be added to the list, I made it clear I wasn't a viable candidate, but would prepare the salad again, anytime. Still, she couldn't resist a parting shot: "Should you reconsider, remember what they say. The first one with a casserole has the best chance."

The Friday before Christmas, we three exchanged small remembrances. After asking about my writing, my family and holiday plans, Ann's focus shifted. They'd received fabulous news Wednesday. After five years, she appeared to be cancer-free. Thursday, everything had changed. Another test result revealed cancer cells in her stomach. Surgery was already scheduled in late January for a skin graft on a leg wound that wouldn't heal. She told me not to worry. "I've beaten worse things," she assured me.

Ann developed a blood clot while undergoing the surgery on her leg. Four days later, all her battles ended.

No one can say for sure whether Les would have really needed Ann's permission to remarry, but clearly she knew her devoted husband and wanted him to be happy after she was gone. Les agreed with Ann's first choice, Yvonne.

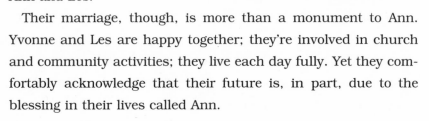

Yvonne is a remarkable woman who had been a childhood friend of Les, and later treasured Ann's friendship. Now she helps guard all Les' happiness, past and present. I recently visited Yvonne and Les at their home and noticed something very special: a glass-covered tray containing the invitation to the marriage of Ann and Les.

Their marriage, though, is more than a monument to Ann. Yvonne and Les are happy together; they're involved in church and community activities; they live each day fully. Yet they comfortably acknowledge that their future is, in part, due to the blessing in their lives called Ann.

Fourth-generation Texan Beth Lynn Clegg has three children, four grandchildren, two terrific "in-law" children and two cats. She abandoned retirement to work part-time for a small software company.

CHARITY IS A VERB

Beverly Hall Lawrence

T he hymn felt so powerful, I'm sure, because I was hearing it for the first time in twenty years. I was sitting in the very pew—the one next to the space heater—where I'd sat as a child and joined in singing "You Can't Beat God's Giving" every fourth Sunday, when the traveling preacher would hold services here, in New Providence Baptist Church.

The more you give, the more He gives to you.

Just keep on giving because it's really true.

You can't beat God's giving no matter how you try.

It was the standard tune played by the pianist as ushers in white gloves passed the breadbaskets to collect what was called the "poor offering." The trustee always explained that this gathering of pocket change from congregants was a separate charity, above and beyond our regular tithes and offerings. The penny-plate offering was to help "the needy," for instance, someone whose lights had been shut off. It might go to a church member— or sadder still, to someone "unsaved" who needed flour or rice for her hungry children. There were some in our community who didn't even make the minimum wages paid in factories, people who had to get by on what they earned harvesting bean fields. The "penny plate" was my first understanding of organized giving.

The more you give, the more He gives to you.

Just keep on giving because it's really true.

You can't beat God's giving no matter how you try.

I felt as if I were hearing the hymn fresh, with new ears. Granted, the sounds that you might call ol' time religion were comforting. That Sunday, it was clear that much of what is within me had been put inside me in this place, the New Providence Baptist Church, in the tiny town of Ashburn, Georgia, where, although I'd been long absent, I was still known. Yeah, I was grown, gone to the big city for the real lessons of life, but I had come home.

Sitting in that familiar pew, listening to that hymn, I realized in a new way that I'd been raised in a culture of charity. The graciousness of Southern "country" black folk is undeniable. You don't have to be born Southern or in the country or black to have a spirit of charity imprinted in you, but it sure might give you a head start. I was grown, but it was here at home, while I was coming up, that I had learned what Plato called the craft of life.

There was no denying the years that had passed since I'd last been in Ashburn for a visit that lasted longer than three days, but to neighbors all around, it was as if I had simply run an errand to the Piggly Wiggly food market downtown. On the very first day I arrived, wheeling a rental car into the dirt driveway covered in a fresh blanket of pine straw, my "real" life began again.

I heard: "Welcome home, sho' did miss your smiling face." And, "Well, is everything in New Yawk okay?"

Two decades had passed, yet Miss 'Cille shouted her greetings across the hedges that separated her property from ours, as if only days had passed since she last saw me. Her mommy, I remembered, used to sit in that same spot on the porch, rocking and spitting tobacco juice into her slop jar.

It was from this perch that 'Cille had called long distance on her cordless phone, up to Atlanta, to tell my sister, Natalie, that she thought our mother's illness might be turning worse. My mom, known to all as Eun, had called her nosey, but we all realized 'Cille was doing what neighborly black folks do: "Looking out for one 'nother." And, all things considered, I had to agree when she asked, "It'n it nice to be home again?"

Yet it was a sorrowful mission that brought me back to the tiny frame house at 105 Story Street, where I grew up, where my mom had grown up, and where my grandmama Maude had died on her knees in the bathroom. Her husband, George, had built this house "with his own two hands" after being fired from his ditchdigger job for being "uppity." This house, in which so much had happened, was now a hospice for my mother who, at age sixty-four, lay dying of cancer that had begun as a mole on her foot twenty-one years earlier.

As Eun's mortality hove into view, friends and neighbors encircled us in their love. I was humbled by the outpourings from those who themselves were poor in everything but charity. I remember the seven single dollar bills that Miss Rose Johnson stuffed into my palm. Her visit with my mom had moved her to give what she felt we needed, "a little milk money." Before that visit, her relationship with my mom had been mainly professional. My mom had been a kindergarten teacher, and Miss Johnson, who said she'd often been encouraged by my mother, was the school's maid.

I was also humbled by the graciousness of the physical therapist, who tried to get my mother into the idea of rehabilitation, after the amputation of part of her foot. Cancer is a slow, cannibalistic illness, but the therapist, a recent immigrant from Manila, thought that certain exercises would give my mother more mobility. My mom just plain refused, saying, "I just can't do it."

And so the therapist and I had chatted about her adjustment to rural Southern life and each of our native cuisines. Some days later, this lovely woman left in our mailbox a dinner's worth of *pancit*, a delicious rice and noodle casserole with bits of meat and vegetables, to feed me, the "on-site caregiver." She'd wanted me to taste one of her favorite dishes. And her generosity was all the more outstanding since she was a newcomer in town.

I am the fourth generation—since 1897—of a proud, God-fearing family of "proper folk," whose vocations as educators and businessmen were unusual in this town of five thousand, where most work was agricultural. It seemed to me that many of the people of Ashburn, whether they knew us intimately or not, were—and had long been—as proud of us as if we were blood kin.

The death in my family would be a death in the town's family. But my mother's neighbors and other admirers were determined that the waiting would be neither lonely nor without celebration of her life, of life itself.

Every day, for nearly a year, as I waited in the shadow of illness, my mother's friends endeavored to do something nice for her and for me—for us. In the seventh month of every-fourth-Sunday at New Providence, I was given the $78.03 collected in the "poor offering." We weren't indigent; and the amount couldn't dent the tens of thousands of dollars my mother's illness and leave-taking would cost. But this was a loving gesture that was of infinite value.

It was as warming as the gesture another neighbor made by leaving three ripened cantaloupes with a note that fresh fruit is good for illness. Another gift was well-meaning, if inappropriate, given my mom's terminal condition. It was a get-well card delivered in person by a woman known about town for her enjoyment of moonshine. During her visit, she thanked my mom for her tutelage when she had just started school; no line of conversation could have delighted Eun more. My mom and her visitor cried together. I don't know what sparked their tears but the crying seemed cathartic to both.

Dying is immensely complex—its practical dimensions, from airfare to food-fare to adult diapers, can be overwhelming. No practical help, no hand extended, went unappreciated. But what I learned that year is that dying is ultimately spiritual.

The gifts we were offered, and gratefully accepted, all translated into something greater: the care surrounding us helped me and my mom make a deeper emotional connection. We talked to each other, really talked to each other. It was in that year that I came to understand what is meant by "charity begins at home."

Before then, I would have defined charity as a handout to someone "less fortunate" or to an organization trying to wipe out a disease. Charity, I had thought was a quantifiable thing, like when my friend Beth gives one evening a week to serve at a soup kitchen. Or when Ted Turner writes a check for one million or one billion dollars to save the world. But now I know that the most important acts of charity may not be measurable.

To live in charity is to attend to the small things that keep the soul engaged in whatever we are doing. My mother's friends and neighbors treated us as they treated most everyone, with kindness and respect—and as I saw my mother, in her health and even in her illness, treat them.

Charity creates warmth wherever it goes. Charity allows you to be open; charity allows you to express love in both word and action. And people mirror your treatment of them. I saw that in my home, in my church and in the town where I was raised. It is a lesson I try to keep with me even now that my "hometown" is one of the bigger cities on earth.

Charity is not an organization, not even a church. Charity is not a noun. Charity is giving lovingly; charity is a verb.

Beverly Hall Lawrence, author of Reviving the Spirit *(Grove Press), lives in New York City.*

SECTION III

♦EMBRACING STRANGERS♦

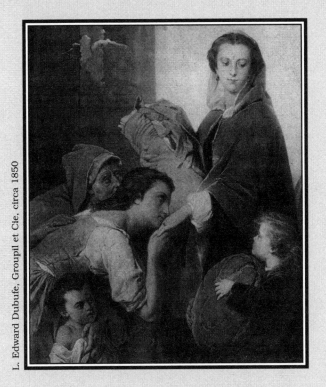

L. Edward Dubufe, Groupil et Cie, circa 1850

"If every person possessing the capability should assume the care of a single family, there would not be enough poor to go around."
—NATHANIEL ROSENAU

A CAN OF CHOW MEIN
Connie Whiting

I sighed and looked down at my bulging stomach. The baby would be here soon. I was eager to have my baby born, yet I was also reluctant, ashamed of the home we had to offer. My husband and I lived in a tiny motel basement apartment: one room with a small refrigerator, an ancient four-burner stove, a sagging bed, a splintered dresser and a threadbare sofa. The carpet was worn through, revealing the cement floor; sunk into the remains of rug was the dirt of ten million footsteps.

A claustrophobic bathroom was the only other space. Looking out its window—a tiny slash in a dull-yellow cement-block wall—I could see the gray stairwell leading up from the basement and more cement. The window wouldn't open, which was just as well, as its malfunction shielded us from the stench of rotting garbage in the old dumpsters at the top of the stairs.

My husband and I also had dozens of roommates, cockroaches who were winning my battle with them for survival.

I watched my husband as he flicked the channels on the fuzzy black-and-white TV and then slammed its side with his fist. The fuzz was unaffected. Disgusted, he clicked it off.

"Let's go out for a while," I said in a small voice, hoping the darkness would leave his eyes.

"Okay," he mumbled. "Let's go to the store. We're out of food."

I carefully sidestepped the needles and empty beer bottles on the way to our old car, which coughed to life after only a few attempts at the ignition.

I knew, to the penny, how much money we had for food. My husband was out of work, and he didn't seem in a hurry to find another job. I would have to be very careful in choosing what we bought to eat.

> *"If a free society cannot help the many who are poor,*
> *it cannot save the few who are rich."*
> —John F. Kennedy

Those thoughts on the way to the grocery set off worse ones. We didn't have a crib yet, and I'd acquired only a few baby clothes. I felt like a failure as a mother already. My husband's lack of concern over our finances surprised me. Had I made a mistake in marrying him? Would things ever get better? For me? For us? For our baby? Tears welled in my eyes but I willed them away with a silent prayer: *Please God, send me an angel or something to hold onto.*

At the market, I selected inexpensive foods we both liked. Then I saw the cans of chicken chow mein. My mouth watered. I could almost taste the tender chicken, the crisp water chestnuts and delicate bean sprouts. I'd craved chow mein during my pregnancy but, because my husband did not like it, I had not bought any. I didn't this time, either, but I told my husband that when things got better for us eating chow mein would be my celebration.

A few moments later we unloaded our few items on the checkout counter. A woman I'd never seen before appeared and placed a can of chicken chow mein with our selections. She also thrust a couple of dollar bills into my hand and said, "Enjoy."

I started to refuse. "Enjoy," she repeated. She smiled, patted my hand and walked away.

I was both astonished and grateful.

Back in our room, I heated the chow mein before eating it slowly. As I savored every bite, I felt my mood improve. So what if we lived in a dump? It wouldn't be forever. So what if I was poor? I loved my unborn baby with everything I had.

My child brought me joy, but the next several years were tough ones as my husband became increasingly abusive. Yet even when I was huddling in a corner, watching him tear things off the walls, or walking the streets waiting for him to cool down—there was one thought I could summon that gave me comfort. I thought of the stranger who had patted my hand in the market and treated me to chow mein.

I actually thought more about her kindness as time went on. Her example gave me hope that there was a world out there where I might meet other understanding people if I had the courage to leave my marriage.

The very difficult years are part of my history now, but the woman's domino effect lives on. I now try to do nice things, little things, for others. Her spontaneous action didn't cost her much, but its value was enormous.

Connie Whiting, who is now married to her "soul mate," runs a business from her Ohio home called Your Invisible Assistant. When she is not working as a virtual assistant, she clicks onto the Healing Hearts discussion group hosted by Yahoo to offer support to abused women.

DANNY'S VISION
Keith J. Bettinger

Some people have a gift for making us see our lives in a different way. Their stories inspire us, opening our eyes to our blessings and to our own potential. As a policeman in Long Island, New York, I have heard a lot of stories, but one in particular sticks with me. I heard it at a December meeting of the Shields of Long Island, a fraternal group of police officers who work for different police departments. This story, told to us by fellow policeman John Carlsen, did more than tug at our heartstrings. It showed us something new about family, perseverance and charity.

John and his wife, Kathleen, had a son named Danny. Danny was a unique child. I don't like to say he was handicapped, because he had so much to give. With his parents' guidance, he turned severe disabilities into blessings.

During Kathleen's pregnancy she and John had been told there were problems. Ultrasound had indicated hydrocephalus, commonly referred to as "water on the brain." Doctors warned the Carlsens that their infant might not survive and suggested that Kathleen terminate her pregnancy. But after discussion, prayer and tears, Kathleen and John decided to have their child and love him no matter what.

Kathleen gave birth on June 6, 1983. Within an hour of his birth, Danny underwent dangerous but necessary surgery. Doctors couldn't guarantee that Danny would live through the operation. Even if he did, the doctors doubted he would ever walk or talk.

Danny survived, but his challenges were many. He had to have a shunt in his brain to drain excess fluid, and he suffered from learning disabilities. His scoliosis (spinal curvature) necessitated a spinal fusion when he was eleven. His bladder and bowel functions were problematic. Danny had little or no muscle control below his knees, and he required the use of full-length leg braces as well as crutches to stand.

In spite of it all, Danny grew up to be a loving, upbeat child. He went to public school and made friends. His happy outlook allowed other kids to regard him as an equal, not as someone to be pitied. He used special equipment to get around, and get around he did. Danny was often in the center of what was going on. He competed in the New York State Games for the Physically Challenged for six years, winning over twenty gold medals in wheelchair races (twenty meters, sixty meters and one hundred meters), shot put, equestrian events and swimming. His friends from school and the neighborhood came to cheer him on. Danny had taught them to appreciate what a person could do, not to dwell on what a person couldn't do.

At age five, Danny had become a youth ambassador for the March of Dimes, a post he held for several years. The job came naturally to him. He had a warm smile and the gift of gab. The position gave him a sense of accomplishment. One perk was that he got to interact with celebrities, including Broadway actor Michael Crawford. And every time Danny's photo appeared in the paper, he would call his father at work and say, "Hey, Dad, I'm famous again!"

Though Danny was different, he and his parents did many things other families do, maybe even more. They went to baseball games, visited Disney World and toured the Smoky Mountains by helicopter. The family didn't hesitate to go out to dinner or the movies, or host get-togethers in their home for relatives and friends. When Danny was eleven, he became the official lighter of his village's Christmas tree.

Before his spinal fusion, Danny endured many other surgeries. His stamina seemed to strengthen the people around him. At the same time, he was sensitive. He wasn't embarrassed to be hugged and kissed in front of his friends.

When his father was the commanding officer of the Emergency Service Bureau of the Nassau County Police Department, Danny liked to visit him and other officers. The police were his favorite "celebrities" of all. At home, Danny would write his own police reports about the activities in the neighborhood. He told his parents that when he grew up, he was going to be a police officer, just like his dad.

One August day, when Danny was twelve, he awoke with what appeared to be a cold. John was sitting on the bed with his son when the boy suddenly collapsed and stopped breathing. His parents called 911, and Danny's heroes—the police—responded. They came in their patrol cars with the ambulance. John gave his son CPR. The officers rushed their friend, the child who wanted to be just like them, to the hospital.

Doctors told the Carlsens that their son had developed a heart infection. The medics did their best to save Danny, as John held his hand and told him to keep fighting. Danny's heart monitor gave a few beats and then leveled off.

John and Kathleen fought their devastation to make a gesture they knew their strong, generous little boy would have approved. They donated his eyes. Doctors harvested his corneas so that the gift of sight might go to two needy recipients. Danny, who always saw the best in every situation, passed on his rose-colored vision to strangers.

Danny's funeral took place on a hot and bright day. School crossing guards stood in formation at the entrance to the church. A police motorcycle escort led the procession to the cemetery. Mounted officers and an honor guard of his friends from Emergency Services met his casket there. All the officers were saluting and crying at the same time. One remarked, "Heaven's police department hired a special little policeman."

A few months after the funeral, Kathleen and John contacted the eye bank and asked if meetings could be arranged with the recipients of Danny's corneas. It was an unusual request, but Danny's parents wanted to be able to tell the last people who had received Danny's help something about him. Eye-bank officials agreed to try to contact the recipients, but told the Carlsens that they might not be traceable or could decline meeting the giver's family.

In the Carlsens' mail one day was a letter from a young man named Ray. John and Kathleen met Ray, who was, indeed, grateful for Danny's cornea. An infection had caused Ray to go nearly blind in one eye, an affliction that was about to force him into very early retirement from a job he loved. Ray is a New York City Police officer.

John and Kathleen believe that their son's most important dream came true. Danny was a unique child, and now in his unique way he is working the streets as a police officer, just as he always wanted to do.

Keith J. Bettinger and his wife Lynn have three sons, three big dogs and a bunch of cats. Retired from the Suffolk County Police Department, Keith is an award-winning member of the Police Writers Association.

A GIFT RUNS THROUGH ME
Deborah P. Kolodji

I stared up at the earthquake cracks in the bedroom ceiling. As my late-summer due date approached, I was filled with foreboding. The cracks caused by the instability of southern California seemed symbolic of my own diagnosed "incompetent cervix." My first two children had arrived early, respectively born after eight and seven months of pregnancy. The fact that I was further along with my third pregnancy—the child was due in only ten days—filled me with more fear than hope.

The pregnancy had been complicated. In March, I'd started dilating early and had required *cerclage*—stitches closing my cervix to prevent a disastrously premature birth.

In May, I had been driving our classic Plymouth Duster to my younger son's daycare group when I'd felt a gush of liquid between my legs. I'd looked down and saw that I was sitting in a puddle of blood. I'd thought of going to a pay phone to call 911, but had been afraid that if I stood up I'd lose the baby. So I'd pulled into the driveway of my son's babysitter's house and had started honking my horn.

The sitter had called for an ambulance, which had sped me to the hospital where I'd learned that I had a placenta *previa* and a partial placenta abruption. But several rounds of testing had indicated my baby was okay, so I had been sent home and confined to bed rest for the remainder of the pregnancy.

By August, I didn't know whether lying on my back for so many weeks had rattled my thinking, or my body was indeed sending me subtle signals that something was terribly amiss. The obstetrician had assured me that the weekly scans indicated all was well, but my largely unspoken anxiety persisted. My husband was preoccupied with work and didn't seem to understand how isolated I felt. My mother, who was helping to look after my energetic young sons, was burdened enough.

In the early hours of August seventh, I felt beginning contractions and woke my husband. He called his father, who arrived to stay with our sleeping boys before we raced to the hospital.

As a lab technician worked on my arm to find a good vein so he could take blood samples, his companionable chatter soothed me.

The delivery was fast. "It's a girl," said the doctor, and I smiled. The nurse put my daughter on my stomach, and I started to caress her.

Abruptly, my doctor asked the nurse to take the baby. In an edgy voice, he enlisted my husband to exert pressure on my abdomen. The doctor barked an I.V. order. I don't remember all of what I heard or saw then, only that I was bleeding too much.

I recall feeling later as if I were in a long tunnel with a distant opening. Every so often, my husband's face would fill the opening as he urgently spoke my name; "Deborah."

Other people asked questions as I floated in and out of consciousness. "What are you going to name the baby?" was one. I couldn't answer these questions because I couldn't find my voice. Then I heard my husband saying, "We'll name the baby Deborah." That roused me because I wanted my daughter to have her own name. I struggled to get the words out, "Her name is Yvette."

When I was on my way to recovery, I learned that I'd spurted blood so fast it was as if a main artery had been severed. In a few hours, I'd had benefit of sixteen pints of donor blood. The human body holds only eight pints of blood, my doctor told me. "The way I see it," he added, "not only did you lose every drop of blood in your body, you lost a great deal of other people's blood, also."

I'd spent three days in intensive care, and was pleased to be able to get his joke, for I realized then that my life had been in the balance.

I was resting in the maternity ward when another man in a white coat walked over to my bed. He put down his tray and, to my surprise, reached for my hand, which he shook. He said, "You've been through too much to remember me, but I'm the one who took your blood before all the trouble started. I just wanted you to know how happy I am that you are still with us. I also wanted to tell you that my wife and I have been praying for you all weekend, and our whole church was praying for you."

Perhaps there was puzzlement in my face, because the technician paused a moment, then went on: "My wife and I went down and gave blood for you."

This man, whom I hadn't remembered, and his wife, whom I'd never met, had given their blood to save my life. Members of their church had prayed for me—a complete stranger—and perhaps given blood, too.

I stumbled out an inadequate thank you, for I felt overwhelmed by his generosity. How could I tell him that his glowing dark face, contrasted against his white coat, made him appear more beautiful than any angel of my dreams?

The next day was my birthday. My doctor brought me a birthday cake, and I was showered with cards and flowers from family, friends and hospital staff. I was grateful to them all. Yet I know—as my daughter Yvette approaches her thirteenth birthday—that the most precious present I've ever received was that from the lab technician whose name I never learned.

Mathematician Deborah P. Kolodji works in information technology. She has 150 published poems to her credit.

ONE SMALL STEP
Grace E. Flecha

My hometown, Portage, Michigan, is small, both in size and in mind. We are not bad people, just sheltered. There are no homeless people in the community and few families of color. Two trailer parks are discretely located on the edge of town. I live in Lansing now, but when I was seventeen, I lived in Portage with my family, and worked evenings at a little coffee and pastry shop off the main street. Most nights the boss wasn't there, and it was just Carla and me tending shop.

Carla wasn't from around there; she'd come from Detroit to go to a college nearby. Sometimes I felt as though I wasn't from Portage either. My mom and dad had moved there from a working-class New Jersey town, and I think I might have been more influenced by their hardship-instilled values than by those of the relatively privileged Portage folk. Nowhere was this more apparent than at the coffee shop.

Each night after closing the shop, Carla and I would have to empty out the baskets of muffins, breads and Danishes into the trash. The next day's pastries would be baked fresh. We thought tossing out perfectly fine baked goods was a terrible waste, but we had no idea what else to do with them. We saved as many as we could, to put on sale for half off in the morning, but there usually were just too many left. We thought of giving the extras away, but by the time we finished closing nothing in Portage was open. So we took home a few each night and regretfully threw the remainder away.

One January day, our boss got a catering order for forty boxed lunches. Carla and I spent all evening folding the boxes and making each individually ordered sandwich. A cookie and an apple were then added to each box. That night there were fortunately only a few pastries left, so Carla took them all. My refrigerator was already packed with two previous days' take-home.

On my way home, the snow was falling fast and thick. As I struggled to keep my car on the road, I spotted something high-ly unusual. Off to the side of the road, in an empty parking lot covered with thick snow, was a Winnebago with the lights on inside. A walkway had been shoveled from its door to the street corner. A piece of plywood, propped up against the side of the R.V., bore writing obscured by the snow.

The next day, our boss called us five minutes before closing time. Angrily he told us that the company that had ordered the forty lunches now only wanted thirty. Carla asked what we were supposed to do with the rest. "Throw them out," he told us.

Carla and I pulled ten lunches from the refrigerator. The stacks of lunches were only rivaled in height by the pile of pas-tries we were also supposed to throw out. Neither Carla nor I could eat the sandwiches stuffed with roast beef or ham; we were vegetarians. Carla volunteered to take home the two tuna sal-ads; her cat would enjoy them. And she said she'd take half the pastries.

I took the other half of the pastries, but there still were eight lunches left. I figured my dad could eat the roast beef sandwich-es at work, which left four. I took them, too, not knowing what I would do with all that food.

The sky was clear and the air was very cold. It took several tries to start my old Turismo. I rubbed my hands together waiting for the heat to come on and thinking about how unfortunate I was to have such a poor car. I drove along empty streets in silence; my radio had died during the frigid day. As I neared the still-parked Winnebago, I saw a man holding up the sign I hadn't been able to make out the night before. It read: Please Help Us.

I watched in my rearview mirror as the man's thin frame disappeared in a swirl of snow kicked up by my car. I'd never seen such a sign in Portage before. I waved my hands in front of the vent, which was finally kicking out some heat.

The next morning, the snow was falling hard again, but it was Saturday, so I didn't have to go to school. My sister and I were early risers, and when I got up I went to her room to tell her about the Winnebago, the man and the sign. I hadn't slept well for thinking about them. My sister said she'd come with me to deliver the boxes of food still in my car. I was glad she'd agreed, because even in daylight I was a little afraid to go alone.

On the way, I couldn't help but hope that the Winnebago had left, but it was still there. The sign was leaning up against the vehicle; the man was nowhere to be seen. For a moment, I debated what I should do. We could just leave, or set the boxes in the snow, and then pull away.

Gingerly, I got out of the car. "I'll wait here," my sister said, handing me the boxes. I balanced them, then looked up to see a little girl's face pressed up against the R.V. window. She watched me as I walked up to its door, and knocked.

A frail woman opened it. "Can I help you?" she asked.

I didn't have a reply. I raised the boxes and said very fast, "I saw your sign, and I work at a pastry shop, so I thought you might like to have some sandwiches."

The woman made no response.

I lamely added, "They're chicken salad and ham, but they're two days old, so I don't know if you want them."

The woman broke out into a huge smile and extended her hands to take the boxes. I gave them to her and she started to laugh.

Her laughter stopped. "God bless you, dear," she said. Her eyes were damp. "Thank you so much and God bless you."

The woman shut the door. After I climbed back into my car, I looked up and saw the little girl wave, then disappear.

The next day the Winnebago was gone.

Grace E. Flecha writes short stories and poetry. An award-winning 1998 poem of hers is part of a mural in Kalamazoo, Michigan.

A BEGGAR OF CHENNAI

David Mason

What roll of the dice made me the healthy one
placing a rupee on his left arm's stump?
I watched him flip the coin from the bone knob
into his mouth with a rueful little laugh
at his own predicament, then beg for more.

Whether it was karma or chaos that parted us,
I drove away with friends in a hotel car.
But I was followed by the flattened look
of the armless boy, who sized the airport crowd
as if in full acceptance of a gambling god.

Soon Chennai traffic heaved from all directions
foot or bullock, bus or motor rickshaw
headlong, woven by invisible hands
so multiple I could not count the strands.

David Mason teaches at Colorado College. His books include The
Country I Remember *and* The Poetry of Life and the Life of Poetry
(Story Line Press).

THE 'OTHER' BRONX

Thomas McGowan

It was about as cold as New York gets, with the icy wind blowing hard. Not a great day to be out. Worse yet, at the advanced age of nineteen, I was recovering from a tonsillectomy. But after I'd spent three days in the hospital and three more at home, cabin fever and the desire to see my girlfriend got the better of me.

I emerged that Saturday from the cozy haven of my steam-heated apartment in the Bronx and headed quickly for my '65 burgundy Mustang. This vehicle was my most treasured possession. I had customized it with dual glass pack mufflers, a top-of-the-line Stewart Warner tachometer, Monroe-matic shocks, and extras from the J.C. Whitney catalogue too numerous to mention. It boasted an FM radio I'd salvaged from a Cadillac and installed in the glove compartment, so as not to tempt thieves. It was a great car.

I climbed in and cranked the engine. It started right up. I navigated the traffic on Broadway and made a right onto the Major Deegan Expressway, heading south toward Manhattan. The car was doing well; as for me, I felt as if I were running on empty.

As I passed Yankee Stadium on the elevated roadway, I checked my rearview mirror and noted a trace of fog. It was a clear, cold day, and this did not add up. No fog in front, but an increasing amount behind me. I checked the instrument panel and found the temp gauge pegged out on the high end. I now knew the cause of the fog. I had lost a hose and was spraying coolant on my exhaust manifold! My Mustang was a fog machine, in danger of burning up its engine.

I turned off the ignition key, coasted through a long curve and made it off the highway onto 134th Street. This put me in a rough

Claude Fayette Bragdon, *The Rochester Post Express*, 1895

area of the South Bronx, a neighborhood known as a haven for druggies, car strippers and muggers.

The street before me was strewn with stripped and burned-out cars. The chunked-up sidewalk was lined with abandoned brownstones, separated by rubble-filled lots where residential buildings had once stood. Any businesses still in operation were closed for the weekend. I knew that to the south lay a blighted industrial area, guaranteed to be barren on Saturday. A more intact area to the north was cut off by a highway. My twenty-five minute zip into Manhattan was about to turn into a long nightmare.

A quick look under the hood was all it took to find the hole in the five-eighths-inch heater hose that ran above the cylinder head, connecting the engine block to the heater core. Using my Swiss Army knife, I cut the hose loose below the hole and bent it back from the block to the water pump in a 180-degree U. I'd have no heat in the car, but this would be a small price to pay for a car that could be driven—*if* I could replace the lost coolant.

My hands, ears and feet were turning numb in the frigid air, and my post-op throat felt as if I had swallowed razor blades. I found a gallon container in the trunk. Now to find water: a real challenge in this part of the Bronx. Not a gas station or pay phone in sight. I didn't know where I'd find one, and if I left the car for long, I was sure that I would return to find my pride and joy relieved of her tires, wheels, carburetor, battery and radio.

At that moment, a tough-looking fellow about my age appeared. Would he give me a helping hand—or help himself to my wallet?

"Yo, man, you got some car trouble?" he asked.

"Yeah, blew a heater hose," I replied, brandishing my empty gallon jug. "I got it fixed, but I need some water for the radiator."

"I can get you some water. Follow me," he directed.

I saw no other choice. With my companion in the lead, we set out, my alarm level rising with every foot gained. I reasoned that walking behind him at least gave me a shot at defending myself if this proved a set-up—although I knew I was not in prime street-fighting form if the going got rough.

After walking two blocks, we stopped in front of a small, dilapidated apartment building. The young man reached in his pocket, and I held my breath, half anticipating that he would pull a gun on me. Instead, he came up with a key and opened the door, saying that we could get water inside.

I followed him up three dingy, dark, and narrow flights of stairs to the top floor. At the first landing, I'd noticed doors fortified New York-style, with multiple heavy-duty locks. The hallway walls were covered in peeling, dark-brown paint. On the top floor, the crumbling plaster was even more apparent. My "friend" pointed to a small common bathroom at the end of the hall, not much bigger than a phone booth. In horror, I saw that the sink was in line with the door, and I would have to turn my back on him to get my gallon of water. I knew that in a moment I would lose my wallet and maybe my life—or simply fill my jug.

Fighting my impulse to run, I steeled myself to face the sink. As if in slow motion, I turned on the faucet. Rusty water began to fill the jug, rising by imperceptible fractions of an inch. By the time the jug was one-third full, I heaved a deep sigh of relief. If my helper were going to mug me, surely he would have done so by now. As my fear subsided, I said a silent prayer of thanks for the decent folks who live in even the worst neighborhoods.

I've jump-started a lot of cars in the years since I was nineteen, and I've gotten many travelers back on their way. I consider these acts but a token repayment to my friend on that cold day in the South Bronx.

Tom McGowan is a consulting engineer in Atlanta, Georgia, where he now likes tinkering with cars in the company of his fourteen-year-old son, Sam.

WHAT'S IN A NAME?

Stacey A. Granger

Heather's mind lay trapped within a twisted, useless body. Born with severe cerebral palsy, she had been abandoned and raised by foster parents, who gave her little attention. She was fourteen, but her atrophied body made her look eight years old. Heather was my five-month-old's roommate on the children's ward.

My baby wasn't in her crib—she had gone into surgery hours earlier for bowel repair. So I sat in the chair watching Heather across the room. She lay unmoving while a tube, threaded up her nose, passed her evening meal to her stomach. The flickering images on a television screen faced her, but what she could understand of them, the nurse had been unable to tell me.

My interest in Heather had a simple root; my baby's name was also Heather.

A nurse bustled in, and I looked at her. "Your little one is in recovery," she informed me with an enormous smile. "They didn't need to remove any of the affected bowel. Good thing we caught it early enough."

"Thank God," I said, and meant it, for I'd said many prayers since I'd discovered my infant listless and refusing to eat that morning. It was one of those "mother" feelings, where I knew without a doubt there was something terribly wrong with my baby.

"They'll be bringing her up shortly," the nurse said. "You are planning on staying through her recovery this week, aren't you?"

I thought about my four other children, spread out with friends and family. I flashed to a worry about how behind in our bills we would be if I missed work for a week. Yet, when I answered, it was with a firm, "Of course."

The nurse looked relieved. "Good. So many don't stay with

their children. This is when they need their parents the most."

I glanced over at Heather. I'd been here for fourteen hours, and the girl hadn't had a single visitor.

The nurse must have read my mind because she said, "Heather is one of our regulars here. Her foster parents just drop her off in the emergency room and leave. We have to track them down when she is being released. They dropped her off four days ago, and we haven't seen them since."

The nurse began to flush the feeding tube with water. Heather opened her mouth in surprise and her large eyes focused briefly on the nurse. "I know, honey," the nurse murmured gently. "You don't like this part, but Nancy has to do it, sweetie." She adjusted Heather's pillows. "How's that? Better? How's about I come back in an hour, and we'll wash your pretty hair and fix you all up?"

Heather didn't respond, but Nancy kept chattering as if Heather understood every word. I couldn't tear my eyes away from the girl's face. Finally, I heard the clatter of a gurney and turned to see a rolling crib being pushed into the room. My little Heather lay terribly still on the mattress. I reached between the bars and touched her tiny fingers. "I'm here, honey. Mommy's here."

An hour later Nancy returned. "Well, how's my two Heather angels?" she asked cheerfully. She washed the big Heather's hair, all the while carrying on a one-sided conversation about how pretty and special she was.

My Heather began to cry, and suddenly the other Heather jerked her head and stared at my baby. "See that baby?" the nurse asked. "Her name is Heather, too."

Slowly the girl reached her arm and twisted fingers toward my Heather. Her muscles jerked and quivered under the effort. "Awwwww," she whimpered. "Awwwww."

My throat clogged. This poor child, who hadn't been shown any love by anyone other than nurses, was trying to reach out and comfort my crying child. I bit my lip and glanced at the nurse. Nancy, too, was close to tears. "She loves babies," she whispered.

I lifted my baby gently and carried her closer to her roommate. For a moment, I thought the other Heather was grimacing as I approached, but then I realized she was smiling—her own special kind of smile. "Awwwww," she whimpered again.

The next day, the gift shop sent free balloon certificates to all the patients. I didn't redeem my baby's certificate because she was too young to care. A few days later, my Heather was discharged, and I leaned over the other Heather to say goodbye. She turned her fuzzy gaze my way, but I didn't think she understood.

The sun warmed my face as I left the hospital with little Heather, and I couldn't help smiling. I was more than ready to get home and gather up the rest of our family.

Passing through the courtyard, I saw a group of wheelchairs gathered together in the sunshine. A gaggle of nurses wiped drool and readjusted legs and arms for their patients. Heather squirmed in my arms as I paused, and I realized I'd been clutching her too tightly.

I gentled my hold and then did an about-face and reentered the hospital. After a quick stop in the gift shop, I took the elevator back to the fourth floor, where I'd spent the last five days. Nancy, the nurse, gave me a puzzled look. "Forget something?" she asked.

"Yes."

Heather didn't notice me at the foot of her bed. I carried the baby to her side. "Heather?" I called. I called her twice more and touched her shoulder.

She rocked her head my way. When she saw my Heather, she tried to lift her hand and gave her smile, "Awwwww." Then her eyes caught sight of the bobbing red balloon I'd tied to her bed rail. Her smile grew wider and a new sound, almost like a soft cork-pop, issued from her mouth. She curled her awkward fingers around the balloon's string. As the balloon bobbled and swayed, Heather let loose her strange sound again.

I realized she was trying to laugh, and I couldn't stay there any longer lest I burst into tears. I patted Heather's shoulder and whispered goodbye. She didn't take her eyes off the balloon.

As I passed Nancy again, she reached out and took my hand. "Thank you," she said.

I shifted my Heather and gave the nurse a hug. "No, thank *you*. Heather would thank you if she could, but I'll say it for her."

Stacey Granger, who lives in Elkton, Maryland, is the mother of six young children and the author of The Portable Mother *and* The Portable Father *(Cumberland House).*

THE HOBO WHO CAME TO DINNER
Tarzie Hart

When hoboes came to a new town back then, they looked for special signs in the windows of the homes. Throughout the '40s and '50s, the image of a smiling cat indicated the home of a generous woman. There was no plaque of a smiling cat in my grandparents' window, but somehow the word got around that the house on Third Street with the big front porch and pink and white shingles was hospitable—I'd love to know more about the hobo grapevine.

In my childhood, I visited my grandparents on a daily basis. "Mamaw" and "Nandaddy" lived on the right side of the tracks in Odessa, Texas, just two streets north of a crossing. When I was little I saw many transient wanderers, but I distinctly remember the first hobo I saw up close. I was sitting on my grandparents' front porch, waiting for the "Popsicle man" to wind his way around the neighborhood in his mobile ice-cream store. His calliope music, like a siren's song, drew all the children out to cool, shady porches and wide front yards. I could hear the music, still some blocks away, and waited in sweet anticipation for his arrival. It was hot that day, in the way that only West Texas could be. The nickel was making my palm sweaty, but I didn't care. A frosty cherry Popsicle was worth the wait!

I noticed a man striding down the unpaved street. Little clouds of fine, white dust puffed out behind his feet as he walked. I remember thinking that he was a man who was going somewhere with a purpose. To my utter surprise, when he reached the front gate, he opened it and came right into the yard.

Nandaddy looked up from the hoe he was using to cut back the St. Augustine grass that crept over the sidewalk. He went over right away to speak with the man. I had already taken in the

"Tramp and His Deeds" by A. B. Frost, *Harper's Weekly*, 1883

man's appearance. He needed a haircut and his fingernails were dirty. His shoes were old and worn out, and his socks didn't match. Mamaw would have said he looked "as rough as a cob."

I have seen pictures of myself at age four and five; sometimes I had a frowny line between my little eyebrows. I am sure I had that frowny look when I was scrutinizing the scruffy stranger.

The man's appearance didn't bother Nandaddy. He had walked right over and shook that man's hand, just as if they were old friends. They talked quietly for a few minutes, and then Nandaddy handed the hoe to the stranger and pointed to the length of sidewalk, yet untrimmed.

The scruffy man began to chop at the grass. We left him to his work and went inside to have some iced tea. My curiosity about the stranger made me forget about the Popsicle.

"Who is that dirty man, Nandaddy?"

"He's a hobo, Tootie," he said. "He needs to make a few dollars, so he's helping Nandaddy do some yard work and odd jobs."

"Why didn't you just give him a dollar? Maybe he doesn't want to trim the grass." There was some lesson to be learned here, and I was trying to understand. After all, Nandaddy gave me nickles for the Popsicle Man, but I didn't have to trim the grass in the hot sun.

"It has to do with the way a man feels about himself when he earns his money. If I just gave him the money, he would lose his self-respect. Honest work for honest pay makes a fella feel good about himself, hobo or not."

I didn't understand abstracts like self-respect, so I silently mouthed the funny word to myself: *Hobo, hobo, hobo.* "Where did he come from?" I finally asked.

"Oh, there's no telling. He might have come from east, west, north or south. Hoboes go wherever they get a notion. Wherever the trains go, that's where they go. They just hop from train to train, always on the go."

"But what are they going *to*? Are they trying to go home?" I asked.

"I reckon they don't have a home. Hoboes live under the train trestles and bridges. Sometimes a few stay together in hobo camps. They build fires to keep warm, sleep on the ground, and drink coffee from tin cans or whatever they can find."

The only connection I could make in my five-year-old mind was to the troll who lived under the bridge in *The Three Billy Goats Gruff,* but somehow I knew that trolls weren't real, and there was something very wrong and very sad about men who had no homes and lived under bridges.

"Beryl, better rustle up some food for a fella who's doing a little work in the front yard this morning," Nandaddy said to my grandmother. She nodded as she rolled out a piecrust, thin as a dime and dusted with flour. It was an art, the way she could quickly turn it over her hand and into the pie pan, perfectly centered.

Nandaddy went out in the back to feed his little flock of chickens. Back then, there was no ordinance about livestock within the city limits. At different times, my grandfather had a cow he milked twice a day, raised beautiful gray and white pigeons, and tried his hand at beekeeping.

Grandmother washed her hands and began scrambling eggs, frying big round slices of beef sausage, and cutting potatoes to fry. She put freshly ground coffee in her percolator and plugged it in.

"We already had breakfast, Mamaw." It was a statement, but really a question.

"This breakfast is for the hobo," she said. "He may not have eaten for days, so I'll make plenty." While breakfast cooked, she stuffed a paper bag with fruit, cookies, canned tuna, a jar of home-canned pickles, a box of saltine crackers and a jar of Peter Pan Peanut Butter.

"Are we having a picnic?" I was full of questions.

"No. This is for later, after he's gone. This will tide him over until he finds a decent meal on down the line." She took a clean tablecloth and I helped her spread it on the picnic table in the backyard, in the cool shade of the biggest elm tree.

"You never put a tablecloth on the table when *we* eat out here," I said, wondering why the hobo got special treatment.

Grandmother got kind of a faraway look in her eyes and pushed a wisp of hair off her forehead. "I always try to make it nice for the hoboes, Tootie, because I always think each and every one of them is somebody's 'Uncle Willie.' " Before I could ask about Uncle Willie, she continued. "Uncle Willie was *my* grandmother's youngest child. He had blond curly hair and the biggest, sweetest smile. Everybody loved Willie and he was Mama's favorite, her baby brother. She thought Uncle Willie 'hung the moon.'

"During the Great Depression, Willie got into a little trouble of some kind, the way men will who are out of work and desperate, and he ran away. A neighbor saw him hop a train that was bound for California. No one ever saw him again. My mama never got over it. She's an old woman now, but she can't say Willie's name without getting tears in her eyes. So all of the hoboes are Willie to me. I give them a kind word, a nourishing meal on a fresh, clean tablecloth, some food for the road, and a little prayer as they walk away."

I didn't quite understand all that she had said, but I could feel warmth like sunshine radiating from her.

Between the ages of five and ten, I saw many men come and go through the side gate to sit under the big elm tree. Each was given a chance to earn his bread with dignity, and good food to nourish body and soul, served in cool shade on a clean, white tablecloth.

The men who accepted gratefully and quietly the charity of an afternoon were never questioned about their lives, though some shared their often unbelievably sad stories of separation and homesickness. Many were silent about their pasts, leaving us to wonder about their secrets.

Never for a moment would my grandparents have considered *not* helping those in need. It was how people were in that different world, when I was five.

Tarzie Hart is the administrative manager of an agency that provides advocacy and services for people with disabilities, and teaches creative writing. She lives near Columbia, Missouri.

BOUNTIFUL OR GULLIBLE?

W e need your help so much," says the sincere-sounding voice on the phone. "I've had people give as much as $6,000. What can you give to help us?"

Is it charity? Or is it a scam?

The link between charity and gullibility goes far, far back. Consider the literary character, Lady Bountiful. Since the debut of George Farquhar's five-act comedy *The Beaux' Stratagem*, in 1707, Lady Bountiful is a description often employed with an edge. In the play, she is a character so generous that she is easily fooled.

The comedy begins with two scheming rakes from London stumbling upon the town where she lives. "My Lady Bountiful is one of the best of women," Lord Boniface tells them. "Her last husband, Sir Charles Bountiful, left her worth a thousand pound a year; and, I believe, she lays out one half on't in charitable uses for the good of her neighbors."

Hearing of her penchant for healing the ill, one schemer pretends to have a fit outside her gate, gaining him entrance to her home and contact with Lady Bountiful's lovely single daughter. Lady Bountiful cures the scammer of his imaginary ills, and, in the end, he marries her daughter.

Methinks that it's a good thing there were no telephone solicitors in Lady Bountiful's day. She would have been a fine target. In life as in drama, it is easier to take advantage of someone whose instincts are generous and trusting than someone who is self-seeking and suspicious that others are the same. Although con men through the ages have known this, it seems the words "charity" and "fraud" have become increasingly linked in recent years, and now reputable law enforcers and charity executives are doing their best to get out the message: Donor beware!

According to the National Charities Information Bureau (NCIB), most American charities consider themselves "stewards of your money," and spend it wisely. But scams do exist, and the most successful swindles play on the most popular sympathies: children, police and firefighters. Caught up in compassion, people hasten to write a check, and not a cent of their donation goes to the charity.

"Think on the Poor" by George John Pinwell, Dalziel Bros., circa 1870

Even legitimate organizations need to be monitored—some give only a fraction of the amount raised to the actual cause. For instance, the American Institute of Philanthropy found that the National Cancer Center spends only five percent of its intake on its charitable services. By contrast, the National Childhood Cancer Foundation spends a laudable ninety-four percent where it should.

To keep yourself from being a victim of charity fraud, the key is caution.

- Beware of charities that sound only vaguely familiar. Often, bogus groups will play on the names of well-known charities.

- Beware of overly emotional appeals that make you cry instead of think.

- Beware of solicitors who pressure you.

- Beware of making cash donations. Write checks with the full name of the organization. Before writing the check, do a little research.

- Find out what percent of donations actually reach the charity. The NCIB suggests that a minimum of sixty percent of funds taken in should reach the charity's activities.

- Don't give unless all your questions are answered.

- For third-party information about specific charities, contact the Independent Charities of America (800-477-0733; www.independentcharities.org), the National Charities Information Bureau (212-929-6300; www.give.org) or the American Institute of Philanthropy (301-913-5200; www.charitywatch.org).

After you've determined that a charity is honorable, *then* it's time to play Lady Bountiful—to give and not count the cost. If you give without being wise, your charity is lost.

VAGABOND'S DEBT
Stephen Wing

Time after time the world sends me

miracles

dressed up as one more random mortal

stranger.

To whom do I tender my

thanks?

I owe a hundred thousand miraculous

miles

to an endless chain of fleeting

friendships.

Who shall I repay? Every heartbeat, every

breath

I inherit from the unbroken lineage of

lovers

who walked here before me.

Where have they all vanished in such a

hurry?

How can I even begin to calculate my

gratitude?

What can I do with all these mortal

debts

that hover round me like a cloud of metaphysical

gnats?

And time after time the world unmistakably

replies:

Take good care of all my random

mortal strangers.

Stephen Wing lives in Atlanta, Georgia. This poem will appear in Crossing the Expressway *(Dolphin & Orchids).*

HAVE A SAFE TRIP
Elizabeth Chase

Excuse me, young lady, I need your help."

I cracked open one eye and looked straight into those of the oldest-looking woman on Earth.

"Yes ma'am, if I'm able."

"Would you help this old woman get on the number seven bus? These old eyes don't see so well anymore."

Could've fooled me. She looked ancient but far from helpless. Her eyes seemed sharp enough in her intelligent face, framed by the furry hood on her full-length wool coat. The bottom of the coat touched her ankles; it would have reached my knees. I thought of childhood days spent with my sisters in grandmother's attic, playing in grown-up clothes from another era.

"Sure, I can do that." It seemed an easy enough task. "I'm taking that bus, too."

"Well then, dear, I'll just follow you."

Fair enough. The Veteran's Hospital had built a heated foyer, just off the main lobby, so we didn't have to wait outside in the wind, which was driving the sleet almost horizontally this late Sunday afternoon. The bus would be here in ten minutes. I resisted the urge to lie full-length on the bench as I resumed dozing.

I had worked both my regular job as a trauma nurse and attended my Army Reserve meetings that weekend, teaching reservists who wanted to be medics how to do basic patient care. My regular shift in the emergency room at another facility would start in two hours. I looked forward to a refreshing nap on the locker room sofa.

When the bus arrived, I roused myself long enough to stumble aboard and slump into a seat. Some time later I stirred; the turns and light patterns felt different.

I glanced out the window. The bus was on the other side of the airport from the Veteran's Hospital, opposite the direction I needed to go. I read the bus kiosk backwards through the screen: Southdale Mall. Whoops—I'd boarded the wrong bus and was at least twenty miles from work, heading farther out.

I reckoned the time it would take me to get to my job and realized that if connections were good, I could still make it, with minutes to spare.

Then I remembered the elderly woman. She was on the bus— the wrong bus, thanks to me. Why had I promised to help her when I was so tired? And what was I going to do with *her* now that time was closing in?

There was nothing for it but to keep my word. My getting to work on time had to slide down my priority list. This woman had trusted me to get her on the right bus, and I had let her down. My dad had always told me to take responsibility for my actions and to do the right thing—no matter what. He'd said, "Integrity is what you do when no one else is looking."

And he had shown his children, by example after example, how important it is to help others. Well, I had promised to help this woman and, having steered her wrong, I had to make it my responsibility to make it right again.

Through the bus window, I could see trash being whipped into frenzy by the dervish wind. The dirty light of the day was going fast. I squared my shoulders, symbolically attempting to exchange exhaustion for determination, and approached the bus driver. His glance scolded me for daring to cross the yellow line on the bus floor. But as I quietly explained my dilemma, his expression became gentler. I asked for two transfers and assistance in figuring out the best bus connections. He handed me two cards and instructed, "You see she gets on the right bus, y'hear?"

I nodded solemnly and examined the unfamiliar cards. They were emergency bus passes, which, unlike transfers, would not expire in one hour, and could be used for round trips.

"Thank you," I said. "I'll see she's safe."

"I know you will, hon. You got that look about you."

I walked back and sat beside the elderly woman. I confessed my error. She patted my hand.

At Southdale, we made our connection to get downtown, then caught the bus to her home. The windows allowed in light from the street lamps and it was in this musty glow that we began to talk, sharing stories of turning mishaps into adventures and unexpected crossings of paths. We exchanged names; hers was Helena.

At her stop I got off with her, although I hadn't exactly known I was going to do that. Helena pointed in the direction of her house. I looked down the three blocks we had to walk. The snow had melted and refrozen so many times that winter that the sidewalks were hazardous stretches of irregular ice. I had taken care of many elderly people who had broken hips, ankles and arms trying to negotiate sidewalks like this, and I knew we'd have to take it very, very slowly.

Helena's diminutiveness helped me steer and steady her, but even I had trouble keeping my footing. Somehow, we were still vertical when we got to her door.

As Helena rustled through her bag for her keys, I asked her age.

"Ninety-eight," she said. "And yours?"

"Thirty-three," I answered. Then I blurted out, "I'm glad I saw you home."

She touched my cheek and said, "I knew you would help me, dear. I knew you would."

How did *she* know that when I didn't know that, I wondered as I made my way, slowly again, back to the bus stop?

Waiting for the bus, I wiped my face with my coat sleeve to keep my eyelashes from freezing together. How others could read me was a mystery, but I realized whose lessons I'd absorbed, who had nurtured the better part of my nature. I peered into the cold dark and murmured, "Thank you, Daddy."

Elizabeth Chase and her husband Drew live in Minneapolis, Minnesota with their two sons and immense dog. Her vocation remains nursing; her avocation is fancy sewing.

SECTION IV

◆Very Special Gifts◆

F. Silber, *The Imperial Highway*, Ilman Bros.

" . . . and a little child shall lead them."
—Isaiah 11:6

A TRUE PRINCESS
Colette C. Trottier (with Michele Wallace Campanelli)

I will never forget Sarah. In my eight years as a Head Start teacher, she was my most exceptional student.

One morning, the administrator called my assistant and me into her office. She told us that we'd be getting a new student— a three-year-old named Sarah. The girl had been abused, she said. Her father had poured a bucket of scalding water down her head, badly burning her neck, back, legs and scalp. She had no hair. Her back and legs had to be wiped down with oil every few hours so that they would not get stiff.

Sarah visited my preschool room the next day for an introductory meeting while the other students were out. Her facial features were petite, and she smiled up at me with innocent brown eyes, startlingly naked because her eyebrows were missing. The back of her bald head was scarred down to the neck. She wore a simple white sundress that showed her burnt arms.

I was seized with anger at her father. Then I worried about how the other children would react to her disfigurement. I struggled to maintain calm in front of Sarah, her foster mother and my teaching assistant. After Sarah and her mom left, I gave in to tears.

"We must prepare the students," my assistant reminded me. "We can't just let her walk in and be made fun of."

"To make a deal about her appearance would single her out," I said.

After much discussion, we agreed to have Sarah come in for a half day so we might ascertain how the children would react toward her.

The morning Sarah arrived, she quietly took a seat. I watched her every second. During playtime, the other children talked to her and

CHARITY WITHOUT BORDERS

"It is not the gift that is precious, it is the love."
—Russian saying

"Give thanks for a little and you'll find a lot."
—African (Hausa) saying

"If you continually give, you will continually have."
—Chinese saying

"Who gives to me teaches me to give."
—Dutch saying

shared their toys. They didn't seem to notice she was different.

"Teacher, it's dress-up time," one student reminded me. Every day before lunch, they all got to raid the closets and play in a collection of grown-up clothes and fanciful kids' costumes.

"Okay, everyone, let's get started," I agreed.

Sarah followed the other children and put on an Easter bonnet and a princess outfit. The disparity between the delicate fabric and her scarred skin made me ache for her.

Sarah left after lunch. Her classmates had naptime, and then I led a vocabulary-building lesson.

Finally I asked the children, "So how do you all like our new friend Sarah?"

One child answered, "Her hands are small."

Another added, "She picked the long skirt for dress-up."

Not one mentioned her thick skin or her missing hair.

The children's observations helped me realize something very valuable. We teachers saw Sarah as a child who had suffered greatly, a child who needed special handling and assistance. We wanted to hold her, prove to her that not all adults were bad. The children, many of whom had also suffered in some way, saw beyond her scarred appearance. They saw another child, a peer, a new friend.

The next school day during dress-up, Sarah put on the princess clothes again. She stood in front of a full-length mirror and danced before her reflection. "I am so beautiful," she murmured to herself.

The confidence of her whirling poses and self-compliment struck me. Here was a child, who I thought, should be shriveling in self-pity. Instead she was twirling around, having fun. I felt humbled by her inner strength and honored to witness her joy in just being alive. I reached out and embraced her. "Yes, Sarah, you are beautiful."

Colette C. Trottier told this story to her relative, writer Michele Wallace Campanelli. Both women live in Florida. Ms. Campanelli is the author of both Romance and Young Adult novels, including Margarita, The Case of the Numbers Kidnapper (*Hollis Books).*

SIGNS OF LOVE
Betty Winslow

After I got married and settled in Ohio, my teenage brother, Jim, often came to visit us in the summer. The large signs in farm fields announcing the type of seed planted in them intrigued him. His favorites were the ones for DeKalb Corn, shaped like large ears of corn. "Boy, I'd love to have one of those to take home!" he would say on each visit, and I had to restrain him several times from pulling one up.

One year, after Jim had returned to Florida, I decided that a DeKalb sign would be the perfect Christmas gift to him. But how would I get one? I sat down with the phone book and began to make calls. After a few stabs, I came up with the name and number of the local DeKalb dealer.

My explanation of what I was after left the dealer flabbergasted. "No one has ever asked for a sign before," he said. "They always just take 'em, and then I end up running all over replacing them!" He paused for a minute and then said, "Young lady, I tell you what I'll do. I'm gonna go out in my field right now and take one down, just for you. You give me your address, and I'll bring it to you tomorrow!"

The next day, the doorbell rang and an elderly man in a pair of bibbed overalls and a faded flannel shirt stood on my doorstep, holding two huge pressed fiberboard ears of corn. Both were slightly weather-beaten; one had a couple of bullet holes in it. The real deal, all right!

Taped between two two-by-three-foot sheets of cardboard and addressed to my brother, the ears of corn sat in the corner of my laundry room until it was time to get out the holiday mail.

A few days after Christmas, my mom called, laughing. "Jim opened the package you sent and started jumping up and down, yelling, '*Oh, cool! I can't believe she did it!*' I wondered why on earth you'd sent him old signs until he explained. He says to tell you, they're the best gift anyone has ever gotten him!"

The corn signs hung on the walls of his room for years, and when he moved out, they went with him.

Jim and his wife and their sons now live across town from us, in a lovely, stylishly decorated house. I've gotten him many gifts over the years, expensive and thoughtfully chosen, and he always seems to enjoy them. However, I'm told that whenever someone asks him what his favorite gift of all time is, he pulls two old faded ear-of-corn signs from the back of his closet and says, "These DeKalb signs from my sister!"

Betty Winslow, a librarian at a Christian K-8 school, has had articles published in Guideposts, Writer's Digest *and other magazines.*

PRESENT PERFECT
Kristi Sayles

"**W**ow!" I exclaimed upon hearing my husband, Terry, tell about what had happened at work that day. "What a gift!"

Every night I ask my husband about his day. That evening he told me about how our friend, Donna Christian, had been showing off a large diamond ring all day. "Oh, my hand feels so heavy!" he said, posing his hand daintily as Donna had done.

I laughed at his antics and wanted to know the occasion for the ring. He replied that it was a gift from her husband, Billy, just because he loved her. But then, he added that Donna *had* done something special for Billy on their twenty-fifth anniversary. She had bought him an almost exact replica of the car that Billy had driven when they had been dating!

How romantic could you get? I was thrilled when we were invited to their house for dinner just a few days later. I pumped Donna for the details.

It seems that many months earlier, Billy and Donna had found the car of their dreams in her co-worker's driveway. It was a sporty wine-colored 1967 Chevelle that was a near duplicate of the one Billy had owned when he'd met Donna. Billy and Donna wanted that car! The problem was that its owner had no desire to sell.

Billy had dropped the matter when he heard that, Donna told us over dinner.

But Donna secretly considered the verdict just a temporary setback. She often asked the wife of the Chevelle's owner about it. Was her husband tired of it yet? A few days before her twenty-fifth wedding anniversary, Donna got the news she had hoped for. The owner was ready to unload his vintage auto. After negotiating a price over the phone, Donna called her mother. "Mama, get my wedding dress and veil out," she pleaded. "Come and bring it by tomorrow."

Donna stopped the story she was telling us to catch her breath. She glanced fondly at Billy, who was sitting quietly, with a big grin on his face. "What happened next?" I prodded her.

"I went and got the title and insurance and pizza. Yes, pizza! We always ate pizza when we were dating, so I got pizza! I got in my wedding dress and drove the car home. I pulled up in the driveway, blowing the horn. Billy came around the side of the house, holding our puppy. Well, he looked at the car. He looked at me. He looked at the car again. He looked at me again. He just couldn't say anything. It was like he was in shock. I didn't say a word to him. I just handed him a card that I had made at work that said some things I wanted to tell him. Finally, I got out of the car and I said, 'Get in, it's yours.'

"Billy just looked at me and moaned, 'I'll never be able to do anything this good for you!' Then we got in the car and went driving down the road," Donna finished. Her eyes sparkled at the memory.

"I always feel thirty years younger every time we go out in the car," Billy said, his eyes on his wife. "It just takes away the years. When I'm inside it, it feels just like my old Chevelle. And with Donna with me, it really feels like it!"

On the way home, I reflected on the pleasure Donna took in having given Billy the perfect gift—not just a car but a shared memory. Billy's delight and the way he looked at his wife also impressed me.

It really makes a girl stop and think: I've got a great guy myself. What kind of gifts have I given Terry in the six years we've been together? Tools, shirts—functional presents that miss out on the fun.

My own spirit of giving has been rekindled. And now I can't wait until Terry's next birthday!

Elementary school teacher Kristi Sayles lives with her husband and children in Tennessee. She invites readers to check out her e-book, The Day I Woke Up As An Ostrich—An Odd Collection for Christians *(wordwrangler.com/kristisayles.html).*

EATING THE WORLD
James Tipton

I was born with my mouth open,
entering this juicy world
of peaches and lemons and ripe sun
and the pink and secret flesh of women,
this world where dinner is in the breath
of the subtle desert,
in the spices of the distant sea
which late at night drift over sleep.

I was born somewhere between
the brain and the pomegranate,
with a tongue tasting the delicious textures
of hair and hands and eyes;
I was born out of the heart stew,
out of the infinite bed, to walk upon
this infinite earth.

I want to feed you the flowers of ice
on this winter window,
the aromas of many soups,
the scent of sacred candles
that follows me around this cedar house,
I want to feed you the lavender
that lifts up out of certain poems,
and the cinnamon of apples baking,
and the simple joy we see
in the sky when we fall in love.

I want to feed you the pungent soil
where I harvested garlic,
I want to feed you the memories
rising out of the aspen logs
when I split them, and the pinyon smoke
that gathers around the house on a still night,
and the mums left by the kitchen door.

I want to feed you the colors of rain
on deserted parking lots,
and the folds of delirious patchouli
in the Indian skirt of the woman
on Market Street in San Francisco,
and the human incense of so much devotion
in tiny villages in Colorado and Peru.

I want to serve you breakfast at dawn,
I want to serve you the bread
that rises in the desert dust, serve you
the wind that wanders through the canyons,
serve you the stars that fall over the bed,
serve you the Hopi corn one thousand years old,
serve you the saffron in the western sunset,
serve you the delicate pollen that blows its lullaby
through each lonely wing of flesh.
I want to serve you the low hum of bees
clustered together all winter
eating their honey.

James Tipton is a beekeeper whose book, Letters from a Stranger
(Conundrum Press), *won the 1999 Colorado Book Award.*

COMPUTING HAPPINESS

Pat Snyder

"H i, Alan. How was your trip?"

He gave me his "Brilliant, of course," shrug and smiled. He *was* brilliant, and from what my daughter Carol said, his smile had curled the toes of most of the female staff at the office. Much to their regret, he had married my daughter. Alan did a lot of traveling, and he'd dropped Carol off to visit me while he'd been away.

"I brought you a present." He pushed forward a large plastic case that looked like it enclosed a sewing machine, hefted it up onto my desk, opened it.

I stood there with my mouth open. A computer! It meant that I could type without carbon paper—I could edit and rewrite and never have to get my fingers smudged again!

"It was free," Alan said.

I raised a brow.

"The story goes that the inventor and manufacturer of these computers is a technical wizard," Alan explained. "This computer really is a very good product. Trouble is, the man is so honest that when someone wanted to buy one, he'd say, 'Don't buy this, wait until the new one comes out. It's much better.' And naturally, he talked himself right out of business. There is a whole warehouse full of these. One of the salesmen just gave it to me."

Even though the desktop-computer age was new, I knew what this small miracle on my desk could do for me. I sometimes did part-time office work now that my older kids could keep tabs on the younger ones, and one of my employers had acquired the latest word processor. By today's standards, it was a great behemoth of a machine, but working on it sure beat having to retype pages until they were error free.

Alan couldn't contain his enthusiasm as he set up the computer and put the floppy program disk into the A drive and a blank disk into B. "Never work on the program disk," he said. He prattled gleefully on about the spreadsheet, how the columns worked, all of the wonderful timesaving calculations it could do for me.

While I supposed it would help me do the income tax figures, my own visions for using the computer danced around the *New York Times* bestseller list. I'd written a couple of children's books and even started a novel. The manuscripts lay in my desk drawer.

Although I used my new computer some, I soon realized that writing needed quiet time, something I had little of, even with the kids in school. I loved the creative high as my fingers clicked on the keys and the delete button erased my mistakes, but I'd feel drained by the time I turned off the computer. My new manuscripts joined the others, neatly tucked away.

The oil crisis of the '80s came along. In Perrysburg, Ohio, where I lived then, the economy started to slide. Then my husband had a fatal heart attack, and I was left to manage financially alone. Another daughter and her husband had moved to Texas, where high oil prices meant that Dallas newspapers still had pages and pages of want ads.

So I followed my children's lead and moved to the Lone Star State.

Thanks to Alan's gift, I was somewhat comfortable on a computer, but I knew I needed more up-to-date knowledge to compete for a good-paying job in the Dallas metroplex. I took myself off to a computer course, which covered the basics of an IBM processor. Alan, visiting again, once more tried to explain the glories of the spreadsheet, but I loved words, not

numbers. I turned my back on the spreadsheet and got a job doing the computer work for a non-profit organization.

Meanwhile, the youngest of my seven children had grown into a full-fledged teenager in a prom dress. She was busy with her friends. After work, I finally had quiet time. The children's stories I'd written still lay in my desk. It was time to put up or shut up. Could I be a writer?

I joined a writers' group, whose seventy-five members met in a building dedicated to the arts. Any given week, as many as eighteen or twenty members would share their work. The drill was that you read for fifteen minutes, then listened to comments on your story with your mouth shut. I was scared and excited when I read aloud a subway scene from a new work, set in the future.

When I finished, there was silence until someone cleared his throat and pronounced, "Well, you can write, but that isn't always the same thing as storytelling. In a story, you have to show, not tell. You've told."

A sci-fi geek pointed his finger at me. "This is set in the future. You can't have an ordinary subway. You need a futuristic rail system."

Later, during a smaller, informal discussion at a nearby Denny's, more encouraging comments were offered, and I heard some friendly comments about point of view, getting into a character's head and, yes, letting the reader see the action. I returned home realizing I was on my way to new friends, and I was determined to keep writing.

When Alan had presented me with a computer, he'd thought he was giving me a good calculator and clean typing tool. He'd been right, but what he really had given me was a gift leading to financial self-sufficiency, friendship and a satisfying second career. Alan's gift was the first link in a long chain of events—the means to a new happiness.

Patricia Snyder of Arlington, Texas, spends most of her time writing and painting. She still attends the writers' group described in this essay, and several of her stories and poems have been published.

NOT BY BREAD ALONE

Verlie Hutchens

I t's cold, Mommy! Marcy whined and dragged her feet. How much farther do we have to walk? I want to go home now.

Jimmy bounded ahead, jumping and sliding in the slush and attacking imaginary enemies.

Their mother, Ginny, dragged the family's empty sled, its runners scraping on the icy sidewalk. That sound, she later told me, reflected perfectly the feelings grating through her as she approached the Survival Center food pantry for the first time.

A year earlier, seemingly secure in her warm, suburban, middle-class life, Ginny had not imagined that that everything could change so quickly. But then her husband left her and moved away with another woman. He stopped sending child-support checks, and she had to quit her job to care alone for their two preschoolers. Welfare payments weren't nearly enough to cover rent on her shabby one-room apartment, utilities and groceries; she was always broke before the end of the month. Although the meals she served by month's end weren't anything she'd admit to her mother, she'd managed to stretch her meager supplies so no one was hungry—until today, when the oatmeal they'd been eating three times a day had run out. Four days remained before a check would arrive.

Ginny felt deeply humiliated to be going to a food panty, but she either had to accept its charity or let her children go hungry. Later she told me that until that day she'd seen herself as one who volunteers, not one of "the pathetic unfortunates" who came to such places, not a pantry "client."

She had to steel herself to open the pantry door and step over the threshold into her new identity. Her children tumbled ahead of her like puppies, eyes bright as they eagerly explored their new surroundings. They zeroed in on the toy corner, while Ginny meekly

approached the woman behind the counter. "What do I do? I've never been here before."

"Fill out this form, please, and I'll be right back."

The woman scurried off to a back room, leaving Ginny to scope out her surroundings. Hand-lettered signs told her how often one was allowed to come and that the clothing on the racks was free to anyone in need. She felt dizzy. The form asked personal questions she would never have dreamed of asking anyone in polite society. Those social rules didn't seem to apply here. She filled out the blanks, anyway. Her kids needed food.

The woman came back to the counter, checked the form and disappeared again.

Ginny retreated to a section of the room labeled "Free Library," feigning an interest in the collection of tattered paperbacks as her children happily played.

The cheerful, businesslike woman returned. "Here's your box, dear. I've put in a little treat for the children. Would they like to pick a toy to take home?"

The kids, who had appeared to be ignoring the adults, leapt into action, squealing and laughing as they tried to decide on the best old toys to take home. Ginny didn't bother opening the box to see what was inside. She could guess, but what did it matter? Anything was better than nothing. She wanted to get out of that place as fast as possible.

"Come on, kids! We're going now."

Marcy gleefully waved a grubby pink rabbit in her mom's face. Jimmy lunged through the door with the plastic sword he'd

WHAT IS THE BEST GIFT YOU EVER RECEIVED?

"When I was eight years old, I got my first pair of skis, Atomic 170s, for Christmas."
—Bob, 18, Massachusetts

"For our fiftieth anniversary, our three children planned everything and the whole family came to celebrate."
—Mari, 77, Wisconsin

"A microphone. I can plug it into my brother's amplifier and sing."
—Kaitlyn, 11, Ohio

"Someone gave me a cat three years ago. I'd been real sick and was just improving. Until then I hated cats."
—Milt, 55, Colorado

"My raft trip down the Grand Canyon—what an adventure. I paid my way but I never would have gone unless my friend asked me. Her invitation was the greatest gift."
—Corey, 41, Vermont

"When I was pregnant, my husband gave me a rocking chair for Valentine's Day."
—Lisa, 42, Louisiana

found. Ginny had never been so glad to get back into the cold, she has said.

She loaded the box on the sled for the long trudge home. Halfway there, Marcy climbed onto the sled. Even buoyant Jimmy whined about being cold and hungry.

"I got a CB drum set for Christmas. I'd wanted it for four whole years."
—Kevin, 10, Minnesota

"My mom gave me and my brother the ranch where we grew up. My grandfather had given it to my father, and someday I'd like to give it to my son."
—Eric, 50, California

"A singing Statue of Liberty. It sang 'Oh say, can you see . . .' It also danced and the flame lit up. It was from a random boyfriend of my grandmother."
—Rebecca, 25, Minnesota

"The baseball glove my dad gave me when I was in the third grade."
—Sam, 34, New York

"When I was a little girl, my aunt overheard me say I wanted to be a nurse. She asked me why I did not want to be a doctor. I replied, 'Only boys can be doctors.' The next day she returned with a gift. It was a doctor kit, and she told me that I could be anything that I wanted."
—Emily, 34, Indiana

"In my case, it was genes."
—Peter, 81, Washington, D.C

Before Ginny could remove their soggy boots and coats or wipe away the icy puddles by the door, the hungry kids wanted to know what was for supper.

Let's see what we've got in this box, Ginny said with more cheer than she felt. It's just like Christmas, isn't it?

Ginny assumed there would be white bread, instant macaroni and cheese, maybe peanut butter. She'd avoided buying processed food in the days when she had choices.

She opened the box and, sure enough, the items she'd imagined it would contain were there, along with canned fruits and vegetables, instant mashed potatoes, breakfast cereal, powdered milk and a couple of lollipops for the kids.

The last item in the box was a brown paper bag, rolled closed at the top. She opened it up, peered inside, and sat down, stunned.

She lifted from the bag a potted African violet in bright purple bloom. Its tender fuzzy leaves spoke to a tender part of her, she would later tell me; its vivid blossoms returned color to her drab life.

Her children probably didn't understand why she was crying as she placed the little plant in the center of the table before starting dinner.

I was the volunteer at the Food Pantry that day. Ginny and I became friends later on, and she often reminisces about that dark slushy afternoon when the unexpected gift of a little violet opened her heart to hope.

Verlie Hutchens, who also writes children's stories, has been on both sides of the charity fence. She lives in Easthampton, Massachusetts, and firmly believes we don't live by bread alone, but need the dignity of beauty in our lives.

Eugene Grasset, 1894

THE GIFT OF WATER
Laurie Wagner Buyer

Mid-winter:

up to my chin in fragrant suds

my thighs red from the hot, hot water,

my sighs slipping out like an old mermaid's song

while I welcome your great gift:

an ancient chipped tub and no ration on water.

For I have washed clothes by hand,

water heated on a wood stove, hissing and steaming,

packed in heavy buckets from the ice-choked river,

the sheets and shirts rinsed and wrung, hung in bitter

winds that chapped my cracked hands, leaving them

mapped with red lines and blue bulging veins.

And I have washed dishes by backcountry campfires

all black char and ash and earth, the precious water

carted carefully cup by cup from a hidden stone

gurgled spring and measured just so, leaving enough

for brushing teeth in pine-patterned moonglow

and for morning's steeped and heady Earl Grey tea.

And I once washed myself standing in November snow,

five gallons from Teepee Creek stove-heated and spared

for scrubbing my long length of unbraided hair,

the west wind iced tight my pale white skin

and pitcher dumped water brought forth drenched cries

that echoed through dark, still, star-rinsed skies.

Mid-winter:

no other gift has ever meant so much

as your abundance of well water,

pump-primed, gas-heated, tap-delivered,

or the clean scoured warmth of my rosy skin

towel dried by your rough, ranch-worn hands.

*Rancher Laurie Wagner Buyer has published four books of poetry;
Red Colt Canyon (Mountain Music Press) is her most recent. Born
in Scotland, she and her husband raise cattle in Colorado.*

SECTION V

♦HELPING PEOPLE MOVE ON♦

"Harbinger of Spring" by Maurice Becker, *The Masses*, 1916

*". . . just give me, instead, the bouquets
while I'm living."*
—LOUIS EDWIN THAYER

SEASONS OF GROWING
Tony Leather

At twenty-six and unmarried, despite several girlfriends at different times, I was at a low in my life. Mother was gone. She'd died a month earlier after suffering a long illness. Unlike the noisy, colorful days of my childhood, before father had died in that road accident, our house and garden stood grim in silent emptiness.

Somehow, apart from a couple of years in the army, I'd never got round to leaving home like my siblings, who both had moved far away. I decided that the best thing to do for my grief was to work with my hands. The unfettered jungle growing behind the house provided the perfect opportunity. I'd promised mother to do something with the garden, if that's what you could call it, but I'd never found the time.

On the first day of my project in chilly, early April, I stood knee-deep in a riot of weeds that mocked me. The wild growths that had been left undisturbed for so many years seemed to resist my efforts to uproot them. The ground, I discovered, was dense clay. My spade grew heavier with each load of upturned soil. The few square feet of earth I'd managed to uncover represented a small fraction of the yard; within an hour I was exhausted.

I stopped to rest, gazing enviously over the wooden fence into my neighbor's beautifully kept garden, an Eden of splendidly contrasting colors. Flowers of all descriptions displayed themselves so perfectly in her garden that, instead of being inspired, I felt defeated.

After some minutes, the garden's owner and keeper, an old lady, appeared. She looked over the fence straight at me. Though we'd long been neighbors, our exchanges had never gone beyond "Good morning." Her walnut-colored face framed soft brown eyes, and her smile was warm. Even before she made her gesture, I felt a tangible empathy.

In her hand was a thermos flask, and she offered me a mug of soup. She poured the delicious-smelling beef broth into the silver cup, and handed it to me. "You like my garden?" she asked, her voice as soft as rose petals. " 'God's Grace,' I call it. I'm Milly, by the way. Don't let the soup go cold. I'm glad to see you out here, but you seem a bit lost. Can I help?"

"Your ground is so fertile compared to mine," I said. "This clay is so wet and heavy; nothing nice could grow in it. Yours must have been the same, once, so what magic did you use?"

She laughed, a sweet, throaty sound, and invited me over to join her in her patch. As I entered her garden, I handed her the empty cup. She put it back on the flask, and set the thermos on her birdbath. She then led me to the corner, pointing at an enormous wooden box, open-topped and filled with soft, brown earth. "Put your hands into it," she instructed. "Hold two handfuls to your face, and take a deep sniff!"

The compost felt good in my fingers, alive with insects of all kinds. Its odor was that of life, natural and invigorating. My neighbor smiled knowingly at my satisfied expression.

"This is what my garden needs?" I asked.

She nodded.

"How do I go about getting it?" I continued.

Milly patiently explained that all gardens need "muck"—which is compost, manure or both. She told me about "green" manure, too—plants that are grown simply to enhance the soil and help break it up. Soil, she explained, is a whole world of living organisms that feed off one another. Good plants need healthy soil, but achieving this takes time.

Milly spent several seasons advising me, teaching me how to work with the soil. Her lifelong love affair with growing things transmitted itself to me with her gentle instruction. That first fall, I built my own composting bin, made out of wood. I lined the bottom with old bricks to help air circulate. "That is vital," she'd said, "for best results."

To the bin I added waste—potato peelings, grass cuttings, animal waste and dead plants—in layers about eight inches deep; then I sprinkled the bin's contents with accelerator particles from Milly's favorite garden center. I built a stout cover, also of wood, and dedicated myself to forking over the bin's contents regularly throughout the winter. By summer, I had well-rotted compost.

From May to August, Milly supervised my planting of mustard to help put the nitrogen back into the earth; from September to November, we planted grazing rye. She said that its large roots helped break up the soil.

Our efforts gradually produced a rich brown earth in which plants would thrive. When it was time, Milly gave me cuttings of flowers—roses, dahlias, tulips, carnations and several others.

Over five years, with Milly's guidance, I transformed my unruly jungle into a garden of which we were both truly proud. Pear, apple, plum and cherry trees stood proudly in a kaleidoscope of flowering blooms, the whole edged by raspberry and blackberry bushes up to the fence, which was covered with sweet honeysuckle and clematis.

We annually shared the departure of winter by delighting in a dazzling display of blue forget-me-nots. The lonely project conceived in my despair grew into a joint venture of boundless pleasure.

Years after our encounter across the garden fence, Milly passed away. This sad time, I had the garden for solace. Milly's legacy lived in it, and as long as I tended the garden it would never die. I also know that it is not only my field of flowers that remembers Milly. Gardens all over town have something of hers in them.

Milly left her house and garden to me, and while this enormous generosity touches me deeply, her most important gift she'd shared while she lived, when she instilled in me a love for the wonders of nature nurtured under human hands. My favorite activity remains plunging my hands deep into the compost, feeling its richness between my fingers and smelling its gloriously pungent aroma. This is my moment of receiving "God's Grace." Milly deserved the name she gave her garden.

Tony Leather's garden is in Lancashire, England.

COMPASSION: TWO VOICES
Rasma Haidri

I cry
When the nurse says, Come

sob-choked
in if you need help

so she hears only silence
the ER is always open

from my side of the phone
and we can notify

and may think me rude
the Salvation Army

an ill-mannered bum
when they open on Monday

who mumbles OK
and they'll pay for your bill

then hangs up
you really should have

before wailing and sobbing
your arm checked out

not in self-pity
if you think it is broken

but for the beauty of people
just come on in

like her in the world
we will always treat you

whose voice is as golden
just come on in

as the cornflowers
anytime

on the scarf of my homemade sling.
you have a need.

Rasma Haidri lives on Hawaii with her husband and two daughters. She has worked as a poet in the schools and teaches writing workshops.

WELCOME BACK
Bonnie Ann Barnett

I moved to rural North Carolina from Los Angeles six years ago. I didn't think I was going "home." But while preparing for my move, I decided to dig through an old family trunk in the attic, and discovered that four generations back my family had lived in the deep South, where they'd been rooted for well over a hundred years. The revelation maybe helped explain my pull to Carolina; it also made it likely my ancestors endorsed slavery—and that didn't sit easily with me.

Life in the "New South" was not as far as I'd hoped from life in the old South, at least it wasn't in my sleepy town. One day I hugged an African-American friend on the street, and looked up to see white folks frowning.

The town was small enough for most people to recognize me within months of my arrival. White townspeople who normally said hello to me looked the other way when they saw me sharing a restaurant table with a black person.

The churches in town were segregated, if not by law then by iron custom.

Still, there were signs of progress. In 2000, an African-American was elected mayor, defeating by four votes the white incumbent who had served twelve years. Some white voters grumbled and asked for a recount, but the election had been fair.

Our new mayor invited the citizenry to Town Hall to speak our minds about how to improve our town. Speakers asked for more flowerpots downtown, the removal of rusty junk piles at its edge, a recreation program and more police. When my turn came, I agreed with those goals but added, "I also think this town needs racial reconciliation."

I paused, hoping to see a few nods in agreement but I only heard the squeak of metal chairs as some of the assembled fidgeted. "I acknowledge the sensitivity of this issue," I went on, "but as a latecomer, my outsider eyes see racial division and pain here. Perhaps we should have groups meet with each other or host a cultural-exchange day. If we talk about our memories and feelings, losses and history, we might just understand each other."

There was, to my relief, clapping. When I returned to my seat, one of my children said, "Momma, I think you got the loudest applause." The next day I was quoted on the front page of our local newspaper.

Some weeks after that, I started a temporary job as an "enumerator" for the U. S. Census Bureau. I was sent out with a list of addresses to check. I was supposed to list inhabitants and get their answers to some questions.

I parked my car and walked up to the first home, smiling at the young African-American woman in the yard.

"What do you want?" she barked at me.

"I'm here for the census . . ."

She interrupted. "Listen, don't you bother my mother, y'hear? We've already filled out the forms, and I don't want anyone around here. I'm not answering your questions. The government is not my problem, and I want her left alone."

I wanted to walk away, but I didn't. I let her stare me down for some moments; then trying to sound friendly instead of officious, I said, "Please tell me your name."

The woman ended up giving me her name and the head count in her home, but her manner made it clear that she gave this grudgingly.

In the garden of the second house on my list was a well-dressed black woman who appeared to be sixty or so. As I approached, she continued to water her plants.

"Good morning," I said cheerfully.

She did not look up as she uttered her "good morning" in a tone that made me feel like a small, bothersome child.

"Have you filled out a census form?"

"Yes, and I don't know why you are here asking me this question again."

"Well, I'm not sure why they want us to come again, either, but you are on my list and I need to do my job. I'll be quick. Will you answer the questions if I hurry?"

"Oh, all right," she said, setting down the watering can and crossing her arms over her chest.

"Is this your home?"

"Yes."

"Do you own it?"

"Yes."

"Do you have a mortgage or own it outright?"

"I own it outright, but I don't know what business it is of anyone but me."

"How many people live here?"

"One."

"Can you tell me your full name?"

"Yes."

"What is it?"

"Sarah."

"Sarah, do you have a middle name?"

"Yes."

"What is it?"

"Well, why do you need to know all this? What good does it do to tell the government what my middle name is and how much money I make and what kind of car I drive?"

"They use all these facts and figures for statistical information to allocate monies for roads and schools. There are many more reasons, too."

She picked up the watering can, and I trailed her, asking the other questions on my list. It would be hard to say which of us was more uncomfortable. As I was getting ready to leave, unscripted words tumbled from my lips. "Miss Sarah, I would like to say something to you. I just found out that my people are from the South and go way back to the 1700s. I don't know if they were involved with slavery or not, but I would like to apologize for them and for any white people who may have caused you or your family harm."

Miss Sarah's eyes showed surprise, but as she watered another plant she said, "Well, I accept your apology, but it wasn't necessary."

"Well, it doesn't hurt, huh?"

Miss Sarah looked up, and when our eyes met I smiled. Then she gave me a grin.

I felt lighter as I walked to the next house.

Every family on that day's list was African-American, and I asked forgiveness from all of them.

An elderly couple responded by telling me about generations in their family; another woman, who was well on in years, showed me pictures of her beloved daughters and grandkids; a fifty-ish woman in her bathrobe told me she was getting ready for her daughter's wedding that very day; a ninety-one-year-old farmer told me about the vegetables he was going to give to his friends; an eighty-four-year-old woman recounted horrifying stories of garbage dumped on her lawn and a cross burned in her driveway.

Each person taught me something. It seemed to me that adversity had made many of the black people in my town strong, and they were proud of what they had overcome. Most everyone added that it was not necessary for me to apologize; God knew the truth.

By the end of the day I had heard stories of slavery and of terrible things endured long afterwards. I was also invited to a fish dinner, and some people asked me to come back and chat any time.

My apology was awkward, maybe even silly — no way could it erase grievous history. The generosity that day belonged to the people who heard me out and opened their doors to me, the people who in differing ways said, welcome home.

At the end of my census taking, I was in my car, driving on Miss Sarah's road. She was on her rider mower and, when she saw me, she stopped its motor and waved.

Bonnie Ann Barnett is a family therapist who recently completed a memoir about finding her father, the circus clown known as Bobo. Her book, Bobo's Daughter, *is available at www.bobosdaughter.com.*

RANDOM ACTS
Art Goodtimes

I'd had to borrow a truck from some friends to drive to New Mexico. Mine was in the shop. Trouble getting parts. Not uncommon, living out here in the rural West.

My friends had told me there was a leak in the truck's transmission fluid. I would know the fluid was low because the stick shift would begin making horrible sounds. But they'd just filled up on fluid, and they thought I'd make it.

Coming home late Sunday night, I began hearing those sounds. Horrible sounds. Like big rocks in a small blender. First I heard it in the low gears, and then, as the miles wore on, even in the higher ones. As I was traveling long stretches of deserted highway, I had no choice but to keep driving, alternately praying and expecting the worst.

Finally, I coasted into Bayfield, a small highway town in southern Colorado. At the Seven Eleven, I learned of an auto shop, right across the street. I parked the truck, grabbed a bite at a diner and walked the half-mile to the only motel in town. Everyone was nice. My luck was turning, or so it seemed.

The next morning, I got up at 7 a.m. to be at the auto shop as soon as it opened. As it turned out, the owner was an hour late. A chance to nap, I told myself, because I was still exhausted from wrestling the old truck into safe harbor, its gearbox screaming at me all the way.

When he finally arrived at work, the owner was a kindly looking older man. I explained my problem. I just needed to have some fluid put into the transmission. It would only take a few minutes. Could he slip me in?

"No," he said. "Can't get to it till Tuesday."

"You sure?" I pled.

"Yep." He was sure.

I was a newly elected public official up in San Miguel County. Public meetings were important, and I had one starting early that afternoon. I had to be back, and I was still three hours from my destination.

So, I got in the truck and started it up. If it had sounded awful the night before, it was about to grind granite into rock dust right now. It sounded so bad it actually hurt my ears to change gears.

I stayed in second all the way to Gem Village, Bayfield's highway suburb to the west. I saw an auto shop of sorts up on a hill. Precision Auto Body and Towing Service. I figured at least I could get a tow into the bigger town of Durango.

I clattered to the top of the hill and parked on an almost level spot near the auto shop, certain the truck would never again move without fluid.

The place was a classic clutter of cars. Old parts. New parts. Packaging scattered about. I found the office and walked in on a young man. He smiled as I explained my plight. Harry was his name. He came out, took a look, clearly willing to help. But he only had automatic transmission fluid on hand, and the truck was a manual. "It needs special gear oil," he said. "Ninety weight."

I remembered an auto parts store back where the motel was, on the other side of Bayfield. The mechanic was waiting for a customer. Said he couldn't drive me himself. "I'll hitch there," I told him.

"Fine," he said.

I started hitching at the highway, walking backwards when I heard a vehicle. Thumb out. I just kept walking when they passed me by. And that's what they did. They kept passing me by.

Hitching is a great lesson in patience. Karma. And the inveterate mean streak in American drivers.

I ended up walking the two or more miles up the Bayfield hill, down across the Pine River Bridge, past the intersection to the downtown, and out to the Napa Auto Parts store. Three bottles of gear oil cost only half a sawbuck. Such a cheap solution to such a huge problem. Was it possible?

I walked back another half mile before I finally got picked up. A carpenter and his dog on their way to classes at Fort Lewis. He had even heard of me when I told him what I did for a living. Politics and poetry. Not the usual match up.

Harry was busy working when I got back. But he smiled when I told him I got the gear oil. Over walked Harry's even younger partner, Don. And Don got right to it. Jacked up the truck. Inspected the leak. Found the right nut to turn, had tools to turn it.

I got down on the ground on the other side of the truck and watched the whole operation. Might as well learn something, I thought, for next time.

Don squeezed the contents of the gear oil into the transmission. Like toothpaste, black goo oozed all over his hands.

Five minutes and it was done.

"That ought to get you home," he said.

"What can I give you?" I asked.

"Nothing," he said. "No problem."

And I was awestruck. I'd been worrying all night, envisioning disaster. I'd gotten up at dawn, walked miles in a morning.

Suddenly everything was solved. And not only that, my solver had done it for free. Expected nothing.

"No, no," I insisted, and gave him a ten spot. The only cash I had.

"Thanks," he said. "That'll buy me lunch."

I started on my way, shifting gears smooth as a llama's fur. I was ten minutes early for the meeting.

Art Goodtimes is a Green Party county commissioner and a performance poet with a booming voice and a wild whisper. He lives in Norwood, Colorado, with his wife and two children.

VOTE OF CONFIDENCE
Heather Pike

All the attention made me feel a little like a celebrity. A new arrival at the St. Joseph's Children and Youth Unit, a lockdown facility for troubled teens, I was a dirty young girl in overlarge, unwashed clothes. For the last three months, I'd been on the nation's interstate system, running from a myriad of abuses at home. Now, thirteen years old and worse for the wear, I sat back on my handcuffs, watching with dark amusement the stir I had caused.

I was small and scruffy with a gamine smile, but I think the handcuffs were the draw. As I learned later, the usual patient admission was a quiet affair, lacking any sort of drama; the parents often went out of their way to ensure this. But instead of tearful parents to drop me off at the unit, I had uniformed officers. And instead of the requisite suitcase carefully packed by my mother, I had a shabby backpack.

I had been caught, after my fifth runaway attempt, on the interstate in St. Louis. My mother had tired of trekking across the country to get me wherever I turned up; she'd arranged for the St. Louis police to put me on a plane to Memphis, where two of my home city's cops were waiting at the gate. They'd handcuffed me and towed me through the airport, then took me to St. Joseph's.

I entered my assigned unit to stares. Its other patients found excuses to slip down the hallways and look at me and whisper to one another. The nursing staff and counselors made no attempt to mask their curiosity, either.

Lori, however, was unimpressed.

I heard her before I saw her.

A wheedling voice called out from just down the hall, "Hey,

Lori, would you come here?"

"No," Lori snapped. I could hear her footsteps as she approached the nurses' station. "I already saw your project, and it looks fine. Quit begging for attention."

The rigid tone of authority in that voice left me in no doubt that the person it belonged to was a worker. But when Lori came into view, she didn't look like a nurse. She walked like a man in a hurry, on spindly legs. Her stringy red hair sat just below her shoulders. It appeared dirty. She was wearing a thin, rather tight T-shirt and cheap jeans. Freckles had overtaken her narrow, long features like kudzu, and her thin mouth was pressed into a sneer. She looked seventeen, but I knew my guess was off; you couldn't, I felt sure, work at a place like this any younger than eighteen.

Lori summarized me with pale blue eyes, direct as a punch in the stomach, then kept walking. The nurses' focus shifted from me and they grinned knowingly at Lori's back. No longer the centerpiece, I pouted and sized up Lori, wondering who had just robbed me of my stage.

Later that night, in a hushed, conspiratorial conversation with my new roommate, I learned that Lori wore those cheap clothes because she had no choice. They were donated to the hospital, and she was in no position to be choosy. Lori was nineteen, and had just completed the "program" offered on the C&Y Unit, rising higher in the patient ranks over her year's stay than anyone ever had before. Now working as a volunteer, she was at a halfway point. A success according to the sheltered reality inside this unit, she now had to find a way to segue into the brutal outside world. I never did find out exactly why she'd been on the unit, but whatever terrible life she wore on her craggy face was behind her. She had no family, no friends, no outside life to return to. She chose to spend most of her time with us.

The "Gold Team," of which I was now a member, occupied rooms on one side of the building; the "Blue Team" lived in rooms off the hallway that intersected with ours. At the corner where the two wings met was an uncomfortable cafeteria chair, occupied twenty-four hours per day by a staff member assigned to "Watch." Most staffers simply sat there and read or dozed off. But when Lori was on duty she took it literally. She *watched*. I never saw her relax.

I had no doubt that she saw everything that went on and heard even more. Her vigilance was spooky, and I hated having to pass her to go to the "Blue Team" wing for anything. Her gaze was unrelenting and unfriendly; there was obviously no way to butter her up or make friends to gain favors and lighter treatment.

I spent my first month in the facility pasting myself to the wall as best I could, trying to find my way about the slew of rules under which the unit operated. If any patient saw a peer breaking a rule, the person was expected to issue what was called a "pull-up." The patient witnessing the infraction would say, "Grip on . . ." and pinpoint the other patient's mistake, in essence saying, "Get a grip on, or pay attention to, what you're doing."

It was against the rules to let an infraction slide without a pull-up. This was considered "contracting": making a silent or verbal agreement with another patient to let each other get away with rule breaking. Contracting was very serious, because once the patients let each other get away with small issues such as leaning against the walls or using bad manners at the table, they might be inclined to let larger offenses, like passing notes or sneaking into each other's rooms, slide by.

Lori labeled me "The Contracting Queen" early on. As slick as I thought I was, she always seemed to catch me when I looked at another patient in a conspiratorial way, and she always knew when I had intentionally let an infraction slip past me. It was infuriating.

Despite my new nickname, which I was secretly proud of, I rose quickly in the peer rank system. I was good at pleasing nearly everyone, even when I was sneaking around small rules, so I easily earned the fourth rank, Expeditor. It was a position of some responsibility, particularly during our "Confrontation Group," which met twice weekly.

Group was held in a large room, bare save for a circle of hard chairs. Within this setting alone, and under strict guidelines, patients were encouraged to confront each other. In the process, we released some of the rage we each held in our hearts, learning that not all yelling and self-expression led to violence and negative results. The Expeditor read aloud paper slips, submitted by the patients before the meeting, which indicated areas that needed to be addressed. I was proud of my new job.

One evening, I encountered a slip on someone I'd become fond of, one of my "Contracting Buddies." With a split-second decision, I hid the slip under the next in an attempt to bypass it.

"Grip on Contracting!" Lori shouted, springing from her chair.

I had thought my sleight of hand was beyond observation. "Let me see those slips," Lori snarled, her slight frame suddenly looming over me. I tried to cover my sin by dropping the slip of paper and stepping on it; my stomach plummeted and everyone in the room but Lori faded from my attention. The other patients, including the one I'd been protecting, slammed back into my awareness with a chorus of howls. I couldn't even speak, horrified that I had been exposed. My careful veneer of authority had been shredded, publicly and instantly, by Lori.

Lori allowed my peers to vent themselves upon me for an hour before she snatched my Expeditor pin off my T-shirt and tossed it into the trash, "busting me to the floor," she said.

For the next few months, I tried to avoid Lori. When an outing was planned, I'd hope fervently that she wouldn't be coming along. Then there she'd be, grinning gravel, her awareness of my irritation stamped happily on her face.

We patients arrived at a skating rink one afternoon with fewer chaperones than usual. I had finally re-earned the third-step rank of "Trainer," which meant that I was supposed to be setting an example to those who had made less progress. Lori made it clear, with a warning eye, that she expected a Trainer to show exemplary behavior and to help her with the others. I nodded in solemn agreement, although I had my own goal.

I'd had my sights set on a curly-haired fellow who was "Head" of the Gold Team—Jimmy. I pulled on my rickety rental skates, headed clumsily into the rink and began following him. A love song from my favorite band, Journey, came over the speakers. I floated in a reverie under the swirling disco lights for quite awhile, never letting Jimmy leave my sight for long, scheming a way to get him in the corner for a kiss.

Out of nowhere, Lori skated up beside me. "Whatcha think?" she whispered. "He's really cute, huh?" she rasped, bobbing her head at Jimmy. I felt heat rush up my neck and ears. Her tone sounded chummy, but past history was shouting at me not to trust this overture.

"Yeah, I guess," I stammered.

"Don't play with me, little girl," Lori said as she rolled to an abrupt stop in front of me, forcing me to awkwardly do the same. "Don't you think I know what's going on in that lusty little head of yours while you're supposed to be watching the others? I don't know who you batted those baby blues of yours at to get that Trainer badge, but it won't work with me."

"I didn't ..."

"You didn't what, Heather, you didn't what?" she demanded, cutting off my excuse. I slumped my shoulders in defeat and tried to roll off to the side a little, hoping she'd give up. She didn't.

"Yeah, that's what I thought. You don't even have the guts to stand up for yourself. Go away, little girl," she taunted. "Go sit down and pout."

I shambled off to a corner, in entirely different circumstances than I'd envisioned. I peeked over my shoulder to see that Jimmy was flying over the parquet floor, oblivious to me. The hot skates came off. The day was ruined.

My doctor, constantly apprised of the goings-on inside the unit, pointed out that I seemed to be more angered by the embarrassment of getting caught and appearing imperfect than by anything else. He also made me aware that Lori had spoken in my favor during a recent counselor meeting, convincing the others that I didn't need to be "busted" again. She'd expressed confidence in my intent to improve. These things were supposed to be confidential, but my doctor was aware of the influence Lori had over me, even before I was. A few nights after the skating episode, I lay awake, guiltily thinking over what had happened.

It was true; I was mad at Lori for sighting my soft spot and ruining my fun. But I realized that what should upset me was shirking my responsibility for others and plotting something— the kiss—that could have gotten me kicked off the unit. Not only that, it probably could have jeopardized Lori's standing as a volunteer. For the first time, I felt shame; Lori wasn't getting paid for any of this, and it couldn't be easy work. I was a selfish little monkey wrench in the path of a good, if grating, person. I tried to keep this perspective as, over the next few months, I began to reevaluate much else in myself. And I knew my commitment to therapy had been spurred on by a vote of confidence from the least likely source.

At last, in my tenth month on the unit, I became Head of the Gold Team. One of my first responsibilities was to run Confrontation Group. My first session was positive, but heated

and difficult to mediate. At the end of the evening, Lori presented me with a fuzzy, footed ball with eyes. "You did good tonight,"
she said.

I looked at her, confused by the gift.

"It's a warm fuzzy," she explained at my blank look. Her smile,
warm and open, washed over me like a mother's love. "Don't let
it go to your head," she said gently.

I smiled and walked away—this time with pride and hope—
away from corners and toward recovery.

*Heather Pike, a freelance florist and design consultant, lives in
Walls, Mississippi, with her husband, lover and equal, Sam, and
their canine companions, Chance and Katie. She proudly considers herself a work in progress.*

ISLAND MIRACLE

Bob Biener

I 'd just sold a house I'd designed and built, and I had the time and money to do whatever I wanted. But with my project completed, and with my latest love relationship just ended, I felt purposeless and lonely.

I reached out to an old friend from college. His advice: Take a vacation to Dominica. I didn't see how a trip to an island, however beautiful, would solve anything, but expiring airline miles gave me the incentive to act on his advice.

After exploring Dominica for a couple of weeks, I felt drawn to the Carib Reservation. I spent a night in the only guesthouse, and after breakfast took a walk along a twisted, sunny road. Through the trees, I caught glimpses of the vast expanse of the Atlantic beyond the rocky shoreline.

Rounding a curve, I came upon three native women with straight black hair and copper complexions. One woman held a baby. The three were sitting in the shade on a patch of grass near a little hand-sawn lumber cottage. The shade looked inviting. Plus, I'd been hoping for a chance to talk with some of the Caribs, and learn more about their island. I walked into the shade and addressed the oldest woman. "May I join you all on the grass?"

She hesitated, but said, "Sit down by us, please. I am Stephanie and these are my two daughters, Cilia, who is eighteen years old, and Athea, who is fourteen."

Cilia smiled at me. I could tell she was curious about why a stranger was sitting with them. I looked at Athea, but she took no notice. Her eyes didn't seem focused on anything, and I observed that her head was a little large for her body. The baby looked content in her thin arms, though, and this made me smile.

Stephanie noticed my curiosity. "Jamail is Athea's," she said. "He just reached eight months. The boy was sick when he was born and had to stay by Queen Margaret Hospital for two months."

I asked what had become obvious to me: "Is Athea blind?" This was all the prompting Stephanie needed. Over the next half hour, she told me her daughter's story. I needed to ask her to repeat several sentences, as my ear was not attuned to her accent and interesting way of using words.

Stephanie told me that Athea had been born with hydro-cephalus, and the pressure of the extra liquid on her brain had blinded her before she was one. During the next year, her mother realized she was also deaf.

Infants born with Athea's condition usually undergo surgery to place shunts in their heads and relieve pressure, but this operation was only available on another island, and it and its follow-ups would have required Athea and her mother to make several trips there. They couldn't afford the operation, its follow-ups and the travel.

For over ten years Stephanie had tried to get help from the Dominican government for Athea's education, but she'd had no success.

Then, seventeen months earlier, Athea had been raped. There was no way to know who the attacker was. An uncomfortable silence followed this last bit of information.

Stephanie made a couple of gestures in Athea's hand.

"Does she know sign language?" I asked.

"I can tell her how to do some things with our own signs," Stephanie said.

Athea stood up and handed the baby to Cilia. Laughing, she turned and walked a straight line to the nearby cottage. I could hear her bare feet as she traveled across its floor. Then Athea appeared at a window and smiled. A few moments went by, and then I could hear light tapping on wood; later I realized it was the sound of her hands searching a shelf. Athea, still laughing, returned with a clean diaper and proceeded to deftly change Jamail on a towel she also had brought with her.

I marveled not only at her ability to function despite her handicaps but also her joyful nature.

Stephanie put Athea's hand in mine to introduce us. Athea felt my arm and then my face and hair. I had never been touched like this before, so humanly. Her inquisitive touch reached right into my heart. I felt her spirit, but even stronger, I felt her potential.

I got to know Stephanie and her daughters better during what was left of my vacation, and was impressed by how much Athea had learned to do without any training. With a teacher, she could learn to do so much more. But to what end? Stephanie wished Athea could get an education, but Athea seemed happy enough just living with her mother and taking care of her baby. If Athea knew there was a bigger world, would she want to be a part of it?

The only one who could decide what Athea wanted was Athea herself, but she was unable to communicate what she wanted. Maybe she would like to attend a special school in the States, and maybe I could find a way to get her there. But I didn't want to make decisions for her; I wanted to give Athea the ability to make her own choices.

I went back to the States to try to figure some things out.

Six months later I returned to Dominica, having decided to move to the Carib Reserve. I had packed all my worldly possessions, including construction tools, a computer, a mountain bike and

> *"Goods which are not shared are not goods."*
> —Fernando de Rojas

reference books. I moved into a tiny plywood and galvanized metal shack just a short walk away from Athea's mother's cottage.

In preparation for my move, I had read everything I could about island life, the Carib people and about deaf/blind education. I'd corresponded with blind and deaf/blind people via the Internet and solicited their help.

The Jewish community where I had lived had set up a tax-deductible conduit for funds for Athea. And, with the assistance of my family, friends and community, I raised enough money to bring a Jamaican instructor of the deaf/blind to Athea.

The teacher, Thelma, made great progress with Athea during their time together in an apartment I'd rented for them in Roseau, Dominica's capital.

I was present their first night there. It was like a scene from *The Miracle Worker.*

Thelma patiently showed Athea what she was doing as she prepared a dinner of baked, seasoned chicken, potatoes and a salad. She demonstrated how to use the stove, sink and refrigerator, conveniences not in Athea's mother's house.

Thelma then took Athea through the procedure for setting the table in the dining room for the three of us.

When we sat down, Athea smelled the chicken and raised her hands to grope at her plate. Before her fingers found the food, Thelma grabbed both of her wrists and put a knife and fork into her hands, then guided Athea in a cutting motion. When Thelma let go, Athea twisted her face, made a hungry groan and threw the utensils on the floor, reaching again for the food with her hands.

Thelma grabbed her wrists again and held her in the chair. I reached down for the knife and fork, but Thelma gave me a look that said, "Stay out of this." She twisted Athea out of the chair and forced her to her hands and knees on the floor, directing her to the utensils. Once Athea found them, Thelma helped her to her chair, and demonstrated again how to use the knife and fork. Again Athea threw them. And again Thelma made her retrieve them. They repeated this pattern several times.

Frustrated and hungry, Athea cried. I felt like crying, too. I felt responsible for this agony and wondered what I'd gotten Athea into. Had I made a big mistake?

After Athea finally found the chicken with her fork and cut it with the knife, she flashed a pout in Thelma's direction, but then she lifted the fork and put the chicken piece in her mouth. Thelma looked drained but satisfied. Athea lifted another chicken bit with the fork and ate it. The anger was still on her face, but I believed I'd seen too much intelligence and too much joy in it before, for the anger to become a permanent feature.

That night Athea learned how to eat with utensils, and I learned that I had hired the right person to teach her.

Thelma expanded Athea's communication abilities and tendered her nearly constant instructions in living skills, teaching her how to cook safely and get around in territory that was not totally familiar.

A few days after the eventful dinner, I saw Thelma give Athea a box with fourteen items in it—eating utensils, ball, string and other items that Thelma had taught her the signs for. On her first try, Athea removed the objects one by one, and got the signs right for eight of them. On her second try, Athea correctly signed each one.

After a couple of weeks, Thelma and I brought Athea to the Workshop for the Disabled, where she could work several days a week making baskets. Annie, who ran things there, took Athea's hand and let her explore the baskets that the seven or eight other workers were weaving. Annie then sat her down with a piece of round hardboard with holes around its circumference,

> "Anticipate charity by preventing poverty; assist the reduced
> fellowman, either by a considerable gift, or a sum of money,
> or by teaching him a trade, or by putting him in the way of
> business, so that he may earn an honest livelihood, and not
> be forced to the dreadful alternative of holding out his hand
> for charity. This is the highest step and the summit of chari-
> ty's golden ladder."   —Maimonides

which was to be the base of the basket. Annie gave Athea a pair
of cutters and demonstrated how long to cut the splines for the
basket and how to feed them through the holes. All the time,
Athea's hands followed Annie's.

Annie only had to show her once, and Athea proceeded to fill
the rest of the holes correctly. Annie gave Thelma and me a look
of surprise. Proud tears formed in my eyes, although I was the
least author of Athea's success.

Next, Annie showed Athea how to soak the cane before weaving it in and out of the splines. Before Athea had finished weaving two rows, she pushed Annie's hands from hers. Athea was
anxious to do it herself.

Athea smiled each time she came to the workshop and started
on her basketry. At the end of the first month, I brought Athea
her pay, half of what Annie had received for the baskets of
Athea's that she'd sold to cruise ship tourists.

Thelma could spend only five months with Athea. Well before
returning to Jamaica, Thelma instructed twelve Dominicans in
sign language and in how to teach other skills to people with
multiple handicaps. One of Thelma's students, Lisa, continued
Athea's education, teaching her how to use a cane to walk on

populated streets and to climb stairs. Athea mastered some tasks more quickly than others; each new skill gained brought a wide smile to her face.

Athea now is a voluble sign speaker, with two thousand or more words to her credit. She can do basic math and read some Braille. She is also something of a housekeeping whiz, who bakes her own bread.

Perhaps the most important thing that Athea learned was how to tell people how she feels. One day Athea, her sister, Cilia, and I went to the beach. Her protective family had not brought her there before, even though it was so close to home.

As we walked on the smooth sand towards the water, a small wave swept over our bare feet. Scared, Athea dug her fingers into my arm. Then she let go, laughed, and took a few more steps toward the water.

After a little while we were running through the water. Athea stopped, and signed, "Like sea, love Bob."

House builder Bob Biener also met his future wife, Sara, on Dominica.

SECTION VI

◆GENEROUS HEARTS◆

Giovannino de Grassi, circa 1350

*"You will make mistakes but as long
as you are generous and true, and also
fierce, you cannot hurt the world."*
—WINSTON CHURCHILL

ON THE FRONT PORCH
George Horn (with Anne Jaeger)

I was dumb. I knew it; my teacher knew it; all the kids knew it. I was like a square cat's-eye marble. Every kid knew what was expected of a cat's-eye marble—but I couldn't roll; I was square. Not like nowadays square—a nerd type. I was a dumb misfit, and I knew it.

Teachers didn't call on me. Kids didn't hand me their papers to correct when we all traded test papers, and the Valentine Box in the corner—I knew there weren't no sweet words in there for me. Teachers would tell us to pair up on field trips. I was the odd boy out. Once, an ugly girl took my hand, and that was even worse. I shook her off, and we walked side by side but apart.

Being sixteen is tough for most kids; it was hell for me. I dropped out of school. My folks said the teachers didn't care to help me. My gramma hugged me like a baby.

There was this scraggly-haired old woman about two blocks down the street. Aunt Polly. She wasn't nobody's real aunt, she was just called Aunt Polly. She'd be sitting on her porch, rain or shine, and didn't know enough to come in from the cold. She just let her cats wrap around her, I suppose to keep her warm. At eight-thirty in the morning she'd stand up and wave to me as I passed her by, and she'd be there at three-fifteen when I was coming home from school. Every morning she said the same thing, "Have a good day, George. The good Lord is with you!" And she'd settle back in that chipped wicker chair of hers. In the afternoon, she'd call out, "How's school today, George? You did good?"

By the time I was sixteen, she wasn't standing up no more when she waved. But her greetings hadn't changed. After I dropped out, I didn't care if old Aunt Polly missed me or not. At sixteen, I didn't care about much.

Edward Potthast, *The Century*, 1896

I knew, from the times I went down the street going to my job, that Aunt Polly was still there on her porch. She sat with a lap blanket over her knees, and the cats on top of that. By then, she wore a stocking cap most days. Folks said she was a recluse, meaning she didn't want nobody about her business.

"Aunt Polly came by today, Sonny," my mother told me one evening. "She's got a walker to steady her now. She says she misses you going to school. Says she heard you dropped out. She's a queer one, Sonny, but she says you stop by cause she got something for you. No harm in you passing the day with her, now would it? See what's that old woman got for you, Sonny." Mom was funny about people; she used to say, everyone's got a reason for being on this earth. I was hoping Mom didn't think Aunt Polly's reason was me. Gave me a strange feeling, her wanting to give me a gift.

I stopped by late, so Aunt Polly wasn't on her porch. Never been up her rickety steps, never seen what was beyond the trumpet vine at her porch. Her green-chipped wicker chair was not much green anymore. I told myself, why maybe I could paint it green again for her, for all the times she waited for me. Yeah, that would pay back for what she was going to give me.

"George, been missing you," she said through her halfway open door. "George, been worried about you missing school. Now you come in and sit a spell."

She took me by my jacket sleeve, near pushed me into a

straight-back chair. "Now see here, George, I'm going to be your teacher now and you are going to learn to read and write and all those things you been missing. Couldn't do no butting-in while you was in school, nothing but praying for you every day, most often three or four times."

Oh my gosh, she really was crazy!

"I knows you got a job at the soda fountain, and that be well and good, but now's the time for you to take up learning!" She spoke loud, like what she said wouldn't soak in if she talked normal-like. "Here's a book. Now, George, you're going to read to me!"

There's something about people: Some you don't care what they think, and others, they just make you want to think what they're thinking. Aunt Polly was thinking I needed schooling. I was thinking she might be right.

And that is the way it was. Every day after work I'd go up Aunt Polly's steps and get to learning. She told me stories of lands I didn't know where they were on the map. She finger-traced the exodus of the Israelites from Egypt, did forty circles in the tan desert and then scooted four fingers right into Canaan land. Another evening, she took a square and put it on her garden ground. I sifted twelve square inches of dirt to find all the little creatures living in it. Then she showed me how to test dirt with colored paper that showed acid for some vegetables and so on. She made cards with pictures on them, like sounds that weren't really like the letters. Stuff like that. We'd burn food on her hot plate to tell which had more calories. Believe me, some went up in a flash, and those foods would make a person fat fast! And batteries and wires, what she couldn't do with them, like showing me how to make a broke doorbell ring, and she taught me the Morse Code in case of trouble.

I dared not ask Aunt Polly how much schooling she had had.

A person doesn't do that when they suspect it might embarrass. She kept at me till I could read the almanac and tell planting days by the moon. She laughed at the Democrats when FDR became president, but made me read everything he ever said.

It was Aunt Polly who told me about how five little girls could all grow in a mama's womb. How they started like God planned, how God gave a different spirit in each little girl after they separated.

We looked through that thing one holds what has pictures at one end and glasses close to your eyes at the other. People jumped out and stood up. They'd be standing by a pyramid in Egypt just like I was standing with them. She showed me how yeast rises the flour and when the leaves lose their chlorophyll and turn brown like they was colored underneath all the time.

Aunt Polly. Nobody's aunt, but the best darn teacher in the whole world. She's gone now. No, not really, not really.

George Horn is a retired Oregon timber faller who now works part time in a plumbing warehouse. Since he isn't much for writing, his wife, Anne, a retired schoolteacher, composed this essay from his words.

ANNIE /
Luis Lopez

MILAGRO ENTRE COMESTIBLES

She was best at miracles

a saint before her time

mujer de milagros la esposa

del dueño

Every time she checked

and sacked the groceries

she caused a candy bar

a pack of gum

or a toy

to appear in the sack

one for each child

by the time

parents unpacked the groceries at home

cada vez que ella ensacaba

los comestibles

aparacía

   un dulce

   un chicle

   o un juguete

en el saco

uno para cada niño

cuando los padres

sacaban los comestibles en casa

This never happened when

Fred

or Ben

or Lupe

or Santos

checked and sacked the groceries

eso nunca occuría

cuando ensacaba

   Lupe

   o Santos

   o Fred

   o Ben

We need to put Annie in the Litanies

Tell the priest	*dile al sacerdote*
to tell the monsignor	*que le diga al monsignor*
to tell the bishop	*que le diga al obispo*
to tell the archbishop	*que le diga al arzobisipo*
to tell the pope	*que le diga al Papá*
to skip the process of beatification	*que añade esta mujer de milagros*
and	*viva*
to add Annie to the list	*a la lista de santos y santas*
St. Annie of the Store,	*"¡Santa Annie, ruega por nosotros!"*
"Ora pro nobis."	

Luis Lopez teaches Classical Literature, Mythology, and Latin at Mesa State College. He is a playwright and poet; his works include Musings of a Barrio Sack Boy *and* A Painting of Sand *(Farolito Press).*

PEACE COMES TO A FIGHTER
Linda Lewis

Why did I sign up for this? It's true that I was looking for a meaningful break from the constant duties of raising children, but how can I possibly help a stranger named Jim? He's dying. I'm a hospice volunteer on my first assignment—lucid explanation for a churning stomach. It's not too late to make a U-turn and drive back home to my comfort zone. I could call the director of volunteers and tell her that one of my children is sick; after all, the four-year-old was sneezing this morning. Or I can be honest, and explain that I'm scared. She warned me that Jim has a tube in his throat. What if it's oozing with blood or mucus?

Turning the steering wheel is arduous with sweaty palms, but there it is, 605 Algrove Street, the home of Jim and Mabel. I park, and force myself up the walkway to tap on the glass inlays of their door. The woman who answers has red, swollen eyes. Her invitation to come inside is muffled through the wad of tissue she holds to her nose.

Mabel sits me down and tells their story, from the day her husband, Jim, was diagnosed with cancer to the day the doctor told them both, "I'm sorry, there's nothing more we can do." I hear Jim moan from the bedroom. It's time to meet my patient.

His large frame needs the length of the king-sized bed. I wonder why chemotherapy stole his hair, yet allowed thick gray stubble on his face. His eyes swim in sorrow.

The nightstand displays a dozen medications, a cup of melting ice on a soggy *Hockey* magazine, and a picture of a strong, sturdy soldier with his arm draped protectively over a beautiful lady who glows with pride and adoration. Though I see a resemblance in the woman to Mabel, I detect no similarity between the young officer and the man deteriorating in front of me. I reach for his hand. His long, frail fingers slowly fold over mine and I feel connected.

Jim shows me his chest, fresh with raw scars. Is he trying to repulse me?

No. He's sharing himself, like a child showing off a skinned knee. I'm able, after all, to look at the tube tucked neatly into his neck.

I ask Jim if he'd like a foot rub. A weak curvature in the corner of his mouth signals his assent. I find an assortment of lotions lined up in order of height on a lace doily on another table. Avoiding the sores between his toes, I smear the cream over his swollen feet. Mabel peeks her head around the squeaky door to ask if she may lie down and rest. My first visit seems successful.

I return to the home of Jim and Mabel every Monday and Thursday. For six hours each week, I listen, rub feet, hold a hand, or simply sit at the bedside. Jim comments on one visit, "Not getting well, am I?"

I answer, "No."

He asks me to get a hockey puck sitting on the bureau and says, "Didn't know they were so heavy, did ya? Got hit in the head with one once. See? Here's the dent."

Mabel returns home, singing. She has gotten her hair done for the first time in weeks. She sings, "Oh what a beautiful morning, oh what a beautiful day, " in a voice that's not half bad, and Jim seems cheered to hear it.

Both thank me with squeezes of gratitude.

I thank them for welcoming me so completely into their home.

As Jim grows weaker, Mabel's caretaking duties increase. She calls me on a Friday afternoon, crying. She reports, "Jim

GIVING IT AWAY

"The man who dies rich dies in disgrace."—Andrew Carnegie

Seventy-two-year-old retiree Eleanor Boyer lived a quiet life in New Jersey. She long drove a 1968 Chevrolet Malibu and was known for her regular attendance at the Immaculate Conception church.

In 1997, she hit the $11.8 million jackpot in the state lottery.

She declared she'd give it away. And she started right away. She eliminated the deficit of her local rescue squad and she donated magnanimously to her church, which used her largesse to buy a new organ, create an endowment and build additions to two schools.

Besides the fact that most people don't win the lottery, Ms. Boyer's donor profile doesn't fit the norm. According to a study by Polk, the typical American charity donor is a married parent, age thirty-three to forty-four, who earns between $50,000 and $74,999 annually.

Most people who give to charity contribute a hair over two percent of their household income. They certainly aren't trying to give it all away.

And then there are the exceptions.

Consider Thomas Cannon, a retired postal worker who never earned more than $32,000 a year. Still, he has sent $1,000 checks to more than a hundred strangers in need.

Om Dutta Sharma and his wife, Krishna, are also remarkably generous spirits. Krishna is a nurse in New York City; her husband is a cab driver. They have two children. While most New Yorkers would tell you what a struggle it is for a family of four to get by on the narrow earnings from such occupations, this pair of Indian immigrants are the sole supporters of a school for girls in their home village of Doobher Kishanpur. The couple told *The New York*

fell out of bed again and I pulled my darn hip trying to help him." More sobs. "The nurse says it's time to put him in the hospice unit. He won't go." Now only quivers, "Poor dear, just

Times that they pinch every penny so that they can send $2,500 every year to fund the school. For them, there are no new clothes, no movies, no dinners in restaurants. But for 180 young Indian girls, there are teachers, chalkboards and medical checkups.

Then there's Matel Dawson, a Michigan autoworker who invested his money in Ford Motor Co. By the time he was seventy-eight, Mr. Dawson had donated more than $1 million for college scholarships. Attending college was a privilege Mr. Dawson never had. As the fifth of seven children, he had to drop out of school after seventh grade to help support his family. Though he is beyond retirement age, Mr. Dawson just keeps on working and giving, working and giving.

Such stories prove that you can be a modest earner but a generous giver. One doesn't need to be a millionaire to be a spectacular donor, but hey, if you've got a million, why not share your good fortune—as Survivor winner Tina Wesson has pledged to do?

And if you've got a billion, so much the better! The world's richest man, Bill Gates, has vowed to give away most of his $65 billion. And he's off to a good start. Since 1995, the co-founder of Microsoft has given or pledged over $22 billion and has formed the Bill and Melinda Gates Foundation, which finances international vaccination and children's health programs.

Peter Omidyar, eBay founder, has also promised to funnel almost all of his $4.2 billion fortune to his foundation, which will help build the capacity of nonprofit organizations to become self-sustaining.

America's mega donors include George Soros, a hedge-fund manager, whose foundation has assisted health, cultural and other programs to the tinkle of $2 billion. Mr. Soros is known for his aid to his homeland, Hungary. Ted Turner, founder of CNN, has given or pledged over $1.385 billion to the U. N. Foundation and Turner Foundation, which support children's health and environmental programs.

We all know you can't take *it* with you. But you can enjoy seeing *it* help others while you're still around.

closes his eyes and holds onto the headboard rails. I can't take care of him." She blows her nose, "Just can't."

When I get to Algrove Street, an ambulance and fire truck are parked in the wrong direction, against the curb. A police car, red light pulsing, is also there. The vehicles are vacant.

Men in blue and beige uniforms fill Jim's and Mabel's small house. Two paramedics hover over Jim's bed, trying to decide what to do. They tell me that Jim is refusing to leave; he has the legal right to refuse.

Mabel reaches out her arms to me from her slump in the corner chair. I ask everyone if Jim and I can be alone.

I know that honesty is my sole weapon, the only approach, one that Mabel is too kind to use. I remind Jim of Mabel's slight stature and explain that she can no longer provide the care he needs. He holds my hand tightly as a tear trickles down the groove of a deep wrinkle and settles on one of the pillowcase's flowers. I hear myself assure him of the warmth and freedom he'll receive at the hospice unit, that he'll be made comfortable and can make choices about his illness. His clasp loosens with resignation.

I tell the men that Jim is ready to go. I wonder if Jim is as irritated as I am by the loud static issuing from his helpers' radios.

Mabel and I follow the ambulance to the hospice.

When I next visit him there, I hear that Jim is a tough patient. He argues with the nurses about taking medication and fights off their efforts to bathe him. They understand, even empathize, but have had to restrain him from getting out of bed and slapping staffers. Jim barely acknowledges my presence, except to refuse my offer of a foot rub. Mabel, who is present, seems to have shriveled with guilt from placing her husband in a situation he detests.

Christmas is two weeks away; malls and baking cookies consume my time. I visit Jim twice more, and feel sad and useless on each occasion. The director of the volunteer program assures me that Jim's behavior is a normal reaction, his anger a natural step in the dying process. She warns me that some patients die holding on to their fury.

Before my family's Christmas Eve feast, I phone the head nurse on Jim's unit. She tells me that Mabel reluctantly has returned home after spending three days at her husband's bedside, but it looks now as if the end of the struggle is near.

My first reaction is anger that no one called to tell me. Then it occurs to me that maybe Jim is waiting for something before he dies. Suspecting this, I cannot sit down to a festive dinner. Despite my children's tearful protests, I leave. Without fully understanding why I've made this drastic choice, I drive to Jim.

Approaching his room, I feel much as I did right before I met him. I might even be visibly wobbling. Am I about to view something unbearably ugly? I stop, utter a quick prayer and step into Jim's room.

The accoutrements of battle have disappeared. The restraints binding Jim to bed are gone. All his tubes have been removed; the hole in his throat secretes pale pus. Jim's chest rises barely and falls.

His cool hand just manages to move a faint finger over mine—I think how strong this man must have been in his prime, what great physical strength he continued to show for so long in his illness. With a soft, damp cloth I soothe his head, face, arms, chest and legs. I bend close to his ear and whisper, "You can rest now. You can rest forever, Jim."

Slowly, he relaxes under my touch. I feel something utterly new in him—he is calm, and I feel that serenity flow between us. Our offerings to each other are complete. It's time to go. This proud man will want to be alone when he takes his last breath.

As I walk in my own door, my family tells me that Mabel just called with news that Jim died. They don't need to tell me. I already know.

In a few minutes, I tuck blankets around my children, and linger to feel their bodies beneath my hands. When did they get so incredibly soft and so completely beautiful?

Linda Lewis lives in Long Beach, California. She teaches "at-risk" teens, encouraging them to write about their experiences and feelings.

A MIGHTY CHAIN
Mary Ryan Garcia

I will never forget the April morning I saw my uncle's face on a television screen on New York's Channel Seven. My Uncle Jim is a Roman Catholic priest and he was headline news because the previous night he had been beaten and stomped outside his rectory at St. Fortunata in Brooklyn, and left for dead. The next camera shot showed the sidewalk where he'd been found. If a car hadn't swerved and angled its beams, my uncle probably would not have been found in time for his life to be saved.

Some priests, I imagine, may seem awesome, authoritative figures to children. But that was not how my uncle appeared to me when I was very small. I remember walking along the beach with him over thirty years ago. I was about four. One of his hands held mine, the other pointed out the boats anchored in Oyster Bay harbor. He was gentle and, unlike other adults, he always had time to talk to children. Monsignor James W. Ryan, my father's only sibling, is nearly eighty now, and still has time for all who need him, relatives included.

I'm the oldest of seven children. My dad, a former Trappist monk, met my mother in a funeral parlor at the wake of his mother. Once married, Dad worked long hours as a buyer for the diocese of Brooklyn. I can't remember my own infancy, of course, but when I think back on my childhood I see my mother nursing one baby after another, almost always surrounded by laundry—clothes to be washed, clothes to be ironed, clothes to be folded. She didn't complain. No one really did.

We were all aware, though, that money was short. Mom bought all those children's clothes she needed to wash, iron and fold at rummage sales or the local secondhand store. There would have

"Monseigneur de Hautecoeur" by Floriam

been few surprises in our life, were it not for Uncle Jim. He is a man who rarely has done anything for himself but has done nearly everything possible for his parishioners and his brother's family. This is the essence of his service to God. He serves Christ through action.

My uncle drove to Long Island each week to spend an afternoon with his nieces and nephews. He would take all us children to the movies or take us to the beach and buy us fried-shrimp sandwiches at the Pig 'n' Whistle snack bar. Occasionally, he'd pile us in the car and drive us to the local five-and-dime, where we each got to pick a small toy. When we were older, his surprise might be a scenic drive out to eastern Long Island.

Father Jim was there for the bad times, too. When one of my teenage sisters was hospitalized, and I was going to college in a distant town, my uncle would do a long circle tour of New York's suburbs to make sure I got to see her, then got safely delivered back to my college. I knew he said special prayers for our family, especially for my sister, and I believed that his prayers went directly to heaven, even if God's answer didn't always please us.

When I saw my uncle's severely bruised face on television that morning, it seemed to me as if charity itself had been kicked into the gutter. I cringed at my uncle's pain and, later on, I hated the young man identified as his attacker.

Uncle Jim was released from the hospital, and he returned to his duties despite his doctor's advice to take a longer rest. He told the journalists who pressed him that he'd attempted to give his assailant his wallet, and he could offer no clue as to why he'd been so badly hurt.

The great irony for me was the knowledge that if the young man had simply asked Father Jim for food or shelter, Father Jim would have lovingly helped him to get what he needed.

Father Jim's attacker is behind bars now, and we've moved on with our lives. When I talked to my uncle about the incident, he told me that the secret of moving on went beyond justice; the key is forgiveness. He admitted that forgiveness had been difficult for him right after the incident. "Now I pray for him all of the time," he said.

The conversation I had with my uncle let me begin to set aside my own bitterness. I wanted to agree with Father Jim that his attacker would "probably learn from all of this and begin to take a different, more positive direction with his life."

From information that emerged after he was arrested, I could see that the man who had savaged my uncle was seriously troubled, but his vicious history included not only what might have happened to him, but other ugly attacks on innocent people. Following my uncle's humble lead, I tried to forgive his assailant, but it wasn't until recently that I finally understood how forgiveness works.

The key was in what an unfamiliar priest said to me during confession. I'd asked for God's forgiveness for my impatience with my husband. The priest said, "You are doing well. Continue to be brave in Him."

The respect for me that priest showed in those words was so cleansing that it allowed me to acknowledge fully how much I needed to be forgiven for my own insensitivities to others. Yes, it was my husband that was in my mind. But forgiveness is a mighty chain with many links, and it came to me that if I wished for forgiveness for my actions, then I must also offer it in my heart to any who had offended me: to Uncle Jim's attacker.

It was my uncle who made me hear the other priest's message. My receptivity didn't begin with Father Jim's example after he was attacked; it began decades earlier when on each visit, my uncle made me feel special.

Mary Ryan Garcia teaches journalism and technical writing at Suffolk Community College in Selden, NY.

THE CRUSADER

Chitra Raman

T he state of Assam in northeastern India, with its verdant forests, misty hills and fragrant tea estates was once a favorite holiday destination. Tourists from the world over flocked to its Kaziranga Game Reserve, the last bastion of the endangered white rhino.

By 1996, the picture-postcard version of Assam had been replaced by a grimmer reality. Whole villages were drowning year after year in floods from the colossal river, Brahmaputra. The state's ravaged economy was further strained by the steady influx of refugees from India's eastern neighbor, Bangladesh. Native Assamese called these immigrants "foreigners," and were enraged by the Indian Government's decision to provide them sanctuary and, eventually, even voting rights.

The stage was set for the rise of a new insurgent group called the United Liberation Front of Assam (ULFA). The terrorists of the ULFA stepped up acts of senseless violence, including apparently random assassinations, hoping to compel the Indian Government to disown the alien Bengalis. Initially, the ULFA enjoyed tacit support from many native Assamese, who shared the terrorists' distrust and hatred of both the Bangladesh refugees and Bengalis from the Indian State of Bengal.

Sanjoy Ghose, social activist and rural-development expert, decided to bring his mission to embattled Assam. Sanjoy, a compact, energetic Bengali in his mid-thirties, had already chalked up an impressive track record in implementing rural development projects. He had recently won the prestigious Sanskriti national award for his pioneering work in the state of Rajasthan, where he had spent nine years helping dairy farmers set up and operate a milk cooperative. He also had shown villagers they

could make more money from their exquisitely woven handi-
crafts simply by taking over their own marketing, accounting
and banking. Emancipating hardworking villagers from the
stranglehold of the middleman was one of Sanjoy's goals.

Sanjoy's last name was a badge identifying him as an ethnic
Bengali. Before his departure, television newsmen asked Sanjoy
why he planned to go to Assam. Was he not scared of the danger? Sanjoy reportedly quipped that he was quite used to danger, since he crossed the street every day in Delhi.

That comment was typical of the Sanjoy I knew. His sardonic

> *"If you want to see the brave,*
> *look at those who can forgive.*
> *If you want to see the heroic,*
> *look at those who can love*
> *in return for hatred."*
> —Mahatma Gandhi

wit often made one forget how seriously he took his life's work.
While my friends and I discussed social and political reform in
the comfort of our living rooms, Sanjoy lived out his ideals. He
rarely spoke expansively about his work. When I once pressed
him for some details, all he would say was, "Why don't you come
and see for yourself?"

Sanjoy and I had been friends since childhood, when our families spent summers together and often took us on weekend trips
to mining towns, seaside resorts and forest bungalows. I remember how, at age eight, Joy, as he was affectionately called, would
sometimes walk away from a fusillade of giggles, consuming me
and his younger sister, to explore a little something on his own.
Even then, he had a definite maturity.

Joy's dedication to helping others is particularly impressive when one considers his privileged family background and education at Oxford and Johns Hopkins. He could easily have opted for a secure office job with the usual material perquisites. Instead, he chose to help the disenfranchised and stoically suffering masses in India's rural backwaters, not by studying them but by living as one of them.

Sanjoy enjoyed the unwavering support of his wife, Shumita, a beautiful woman who shared his ideals and became an active partner in his projects. They had two children.

Sanjoy and Shumita's destination was the Assamese island of Majuli, the world's largest river island. The Brahmaputra had devoured 500 square kilometers of the island in twenty years. Government compensation to the villagers was either slow or nonexistent. Residents regularly rebuilt their homes, hoping the gift of alluvial silt when the waters receded would help make up for their loss. But by the mid '90s, most losses caused by erosion were permanent.

When the river flowed against an almost perpendicular bank, it sliced in. This created an overhang that eventually crashed into the water. Sanjoy's organization, AVARD, campaigned to mobilize a volunteer workforce to construct an embankment.

Eventually, 30,000 men, women and children gathered to place sandbags along the riverbank and plant a selection of local species to hold in the soil. To the locals, it was an unprecedented example of what ordinary people working together for a common goal could achieve under the right kind of supervision—with or without governmental largesse.

Focused as Sanjoy and Shumita were on improving the lot of the grateful Majuli residents, they were underestimating the malevolent forces silently aligning against them.

The couple published a newsletter in Assamese called "Dweep Aalok" or "Island News." It became instantly popular as a source of articles on self-employment and on using available government programs. But its investigative journalism also exposed misuse of authority and nepotism by the local political heavyweights. One local leader who had awarded building contracts to her son was exposed, as was the leader of a student union who had helped himself illegally to a tube well.

Although Sanjoy and Shumita's success in protecting a one-and-seven-tenths-kilometer stretch of river bank was exhilarating for some locals' morale, it alienated Sanjoy from the powerful whose lavish lifestyles depended on the inequalities of the status quo. The villagers' new self-sufficiency and solidarity was a serious threat.

On July 4, 1997, Sanjoy and a colleague went voluntarily to a meeting called by the ULFA. The ostensible purpose of the meeting was to discuss the well-being of the Assamese.

It was a trap. His colleague returned to the island a few days later. Sanjoy is still missing.

Five agonizing days after Sanjoy disappeared, ULFA leader Paresh Barua admitted to "arresting" Sanjoy. He claimed that Sanjoy had been inciting the people of Assam against the ULFA and also had been working on behalf of the Indian Army—such charges are absurd.

I learned of the abduction of Sanjoy a full week after it happened. Sitting half a world away in Michigan, I sat up half the night drafting a letter to then Vice-President Al Gore, explaining the situation and appealing for U.S. intervention or, at the very least, strong censure. "Sanjoy may not be a U.S. citizen," I wrote, "but he is a world-class citizen." The letter was routed through my senator. Mother Theresa signed a personal appeal for Sanjoy's safe return. Amnesty International added its voice.

On July 22, Shumita was awakened at midnight to the terrible news that an intercepted fax from the ULFA stated that her husband had drowned in the Brahmaputra. This was later contradicted by another UFLA message asserting that Sanjoy was alive and well in its custody. On August 4, the ULFA stated through the press that Sanjoy had fallen off a cliff to his death, in trying to escape. Later that same month, a ULFA member in police custody claimed that his group had done away with Sanjoy on the very date of his abduction, July 4.

For Shumita, the months of July and August 1997 were "like living on an emotional trapeze." Still, without conclusive proof to the contrary, Sanjoy's family steadfastly hopes that their Joy is still alive and will return to them some day.

I hear friends say: If this could happen to someone like Joy, who in their right mind would want to take initiative anymore? I think they are missing the point. The more significant truth is that someone like Sanjoy happened in our lives, and affected the lives of so many others. Humanity could learn much from the way Sanjoy exercised his freedom of choice. Joy chose to give unstintingly of himself.

Chitra Raman lives in Grosse Pointe, Michigan, with her husband and ten-year-old daughter. In India, she was involved in theater; today she writes on political, educational and technical subjects.

SECTION VII

♦SEASON FOR GIVING♦

"If Virtue feeble were, Heaven itself
would stoop to her."
—JOHN MILTON

IF THE SHOE FITS
Rusty Fischer

I t was cold out, and I needed new shoes. That's really how it all started. I had moved to take a new job, and I still didn't have enough vacation days or money to go home for Thanksgiving. Not having been in North Carolina long enough to make close friends, I resigned myself to spending the holiday alone.

The evening before Thanksgiving was cold and gray, and I was feeling three shades of blue. I left work and decided to take a walk before returning to my lonely apartment. To give myself a destination, I decided to go to the grocery store for a cup of coffee. At least it would warm me up.

The rundown shopping center close to where I worked had a no-name grocery, a dollar store, one of those places that cashes checks, a pet shop, and a Pic 'n' Save shoe store.

"How ya doing, brother?" came a booming voice as I approached the shabby strip. A huge black man in a too-tight coat gripped my hand. "No sir, I'm not selling a single solitary thing," he insisted. "I'm just spreading the good word about Harvest House, a simple little place me and nine other down-on-our-luck gentlemen like to call home."

He let go of my hand and gave me a folded pamphlet. "Would you care to make a donation and help make our holiday a little more thankful?"

I looked up at his warm, green eyes and broad, bright smile. Something about him reached me. His weathered face, ill-fitting coat and particularly his beat-up shoes made me appreciate the life I led, and I reached for my wallet, quickly thinking over the expenses I'd incur before my next paycheck.

There was change in my pocket for the coffee, and I could always charge the shoes and a couple of pizzas I'd planned for the long weekend ahead, so I gave him what cash I had.

His eyes lit up as I dropped two fives and a single dollar bill into his grimy plastic jar full of dull pennies and bright quarters. "Now that's what I'm talking 'bout," he shouted as he clapped me on the back. "Happy Thanksgiving, brother."

As I waited for the listless teenager behind the deli counter to brew up a fresh pot of "gourmet" coffee, I perused the modest Harvest House brochure. What this homeless residence hoped to harvest was the human spirit. One somber paragraph talked about "casting our net out into the sea of doomed lives and reeling in lost souls."

There was a picture of Harvest House on the brochure's cover. It looked barely big enough to hold the gentle giant I'd met outside, let alone nine other weary men.

I read of the home's morning scripture classes and its daily work program, and of how the men pooled their small paychecks for such necessities as toothpaste and milk. Their curfew was 8 p.m., and lights-out was at ten every night!

I don't know why that flimsy brochure comforted me so. Yet it did. Maybe it was the way it brought life down to basics: a Bible verse and a cup of coffee in the morning; hard, honest work during the day; a roof over your head and a safe bed to sleep in.

By the time I paid for my steaming cup of "Vanilla Mocha Java," I was so warm inside I didn't need it anymore.

"Now this is TOO much," shouted the friendly giant as I handed him the steaming styrofoam cup. "I can't accept this!"

Sneaking a peek back at him a few steps away, I saw him taking his first tentative sip.

Inside the shoe store, Christmas carols were already playing. In the section marked "Clearance," shoes were on offer for $9.99. I tried on a pair, and looked at the ridiculous blue racing stripes in the ankle-high mirror bolted to the floor. But they were comfortable. How firm and solid on my feet. I made a mental leap from my feet to those of the weary traveler I'd just met—if these shoes felt like heaven to me, how much more welcome would they be on feet that had supported heavier burdens than mine?

I said a short prayer that my credit card company had processed my last payment. Then I tried to estimate what size the enormous man outside the grocery store might wear. "Excuse me," I asked the pleasant cashier behind her *Jet* magazine, "do you have these in a size fourteen? Extra-wide?"

I borrowed a shopping cart, loaded it with ten pairs of cheap running shoes, pushed my haul to my apartment and loaded the boxes into my car.

I had just enough quarters in my car ashtray to pick up a drive-thru dinner at Taco Bell. I threw the bag of fast food into the backseat, next to the boxes of new shoes. The spicy smells made my empty stomach rumble as I looked for the address on the Harvest House brochure.

I stopped at a dimly lit gas station for directions. The old man behind the counter spent nearly ten minutes recounting the history of the street where I stood, before drawing me a map to where I was headed, a map that reminded me of a pirate's crude guide to lost treasure.

It was so dark outside the gas station that I didn't notice the shattered glass of my rear window until it crunched beneath my feet. Whoever had broken the window had also taken every single pair of shoes. The thief had even stolen my spicy soft tacos!

Inexplicably, I drove to Harvest House, anyway, although I had nothing to give the men now. As it turned out, I needn't have worried.

"There he is," said the mountainous man when I knocked on the flimsy front door. "Mr. Big Spender. What a nice surprise! And just in time for dinner."

Before I could explain my miserable failure, his oak-solid arm had whisked me into a warm, inviting dining room full of smiling faces and hands clasped in preparation for saying grace.

"We've got a visitor," the big man said, and all eyes focused on me, seemingly waiting for me to speak.

I grunted something that might have sounded like "shoes," but it was quickly lost as tears started to stream from my eyes. How could I tell them about the shoes and what I thought they might have meant to them? How could I tell them it would be another month before I could save up the money to buy them new ones? How could I tell them that I didn't even have enough money for dinner that night?

Ten pairs of arms came to my rescue. The men patted my back and said reassuring things like, "We know, man," and "We've all been there, son." I sniffled and snuffed and tried to explain, but they wouldn't have any of it. Instead, they welcomed me to their table as if they'd been expecting me.

There was only one catch. "The new guy," said the big man, "has to say grace."

"Dear God," I prayed. "Thank you not only for the food we are about to eat, but also for the new friends we are about to share it with."

Rusty Fischer lives in Orlando, Florida. His story, "Fireplug," *appears in the Virtue Victorious volume,* Fortitude: True Stories of True Grit.

A THANKSGIVING BLOSSOM
Nanette Thorsen-Snipes

My husband had helped me start the small turkey, then settled himself on the recliner. A rush of anger heated my cheeks.

As if he had felt the rush, he looked up from the sports page. "Do you need any help?" he asked.

"No," I answered tersely. I tossed a peeled egg into a pan and tried not to indulge my self-pity. But it had lodged in me. I picked up the hospital bracelet my teenage daughter had left on the counter before curling up in pain on the sofa, and I flung it in the trash.

Just two mornings before, I had rushed Jamie to the emergency room. I'd stood beside her for hours, wondering what was causing her severe stomach pains. The emergency room doctor had poked, prodded and tested my daughter as she continued to double over in pain, frequently retching into a plastic pan. One by one, the doctor ruled out ulcers, kidney problems, stomach virus and pelvic infection. About mid-day, I felt relieved to see our family doctor. He gingerly felt Jamie's abdomen, causing her to shrink from his hand. I noticed he kept coming back to her right side, watching her reaction. Finally, he stepped back and told me he thought it was her appendix. By 9 p.m., the doctor had removed Jamie's inflamed appendix. While her problem had disappeared on the operating table, old ones of mine had flared up in my mind.

We had planned to spend the holiday at my oldest son's house. I had hoped that the bustling activities of the day would keep me busy—so busy I wouldn't remember that Thanksgiving was the time of year my former husband, my older boys' father, had committed suicide. But Jamie's surgery had rendered her unable to

> **A Thanksgiving**
>
> *Lord for the erring thought*
> *Not into evil wrought:*
> *Lord for the wicked will*
> *Betrayed and baffled still:*
> *For the heart from itself kept,*
> *Our thanksgiving accept.*
>
> —William Dean Howells

make the one-hour trip to my son's. Now, with too much quiet, the memory pushed past the edge of my mind.

I stood at the kitchen sink, my head pounding. I dialed my next-door neighbor, Donna. "Do you have any aspirin?" I asked, trying to keep my voice steady.

"No, but I'll be glad to pick up some for you," she said cheerily, adding that she had to go to the store anyway.

I sighed. "That's all right. I really need to get out." My voice cracked a bit and I added, "This is just not a good day for me." I hung up the phone. Thanksgiving? What a joke. I couldn't think of anything to be thankful for.

Alone, I drove to the store, my nose red from crying. I'd had too little sleep; my spirit was weary, too. I wondered how I would ever make this small Thanksgiving come together for my family.

Self-pity had knocked my energy level to rock bottom. I shuffled like an old woman through the grocery aisles and stood for a long time in the pain reliever section, trying to decide which brand to buy. By the time I approached my house, I just wanted to crawl into bed.

Pulling into the carport, I noticed a new little pot of gaily-wrapped lavender flowers beside my back door. Jamie is so well loved, I thought. Now, that was something to be thankful for. Yesterday, my daughter's friends had shown up with flowers, teddy bears and videos, and I had appreciated their kindness. I brought the new flowers inside and set them on a table.

To my surprise, the simple white piece of paper in the flowerpot had my name on it. Below my name, it read, "God's strength is perfect when our strength is gone."

As I turned the paper over, I saw it was from my neighbor, Donna, who was busy with a large family gathering. The heaviness in my heart began to lift. Of course, I thought, my neighbor is right.

I touched the soft lavender petals, thinking how self-absorbed I'd been. "Thank you, Lord," I whispered, "for a neighbor like Donna." And I felt gratitude start to trickle back into my day.

My husband must have sensed the change in me, because when I returned to my pan of eggs, he joined me and started shelling. The smell of the roasting turkey wafted through the room. He placed his arm around me and kissed my cheek. My heart overflowed with thanks.

Nanette Thorsen-Snipes has written hundreds of articles and devotions for magazines and books, including Home Life *and* Chicken Soup for the Christian Family Soul. *She lives in Buford, Georgia.*

FESTIVAL OF LIGHTS
Manuel E. Kadish

I t was a blustering December day in Montreal. Snowplows had cleared masses of newly fallen snow, leaving piles three to four feet high between roads and sidewalks. I joined other small boys throwing snowballs and pushing classmates into the snow piles as we wended our ways home from school. After my playmates veered off on different routes, a classmate I barely knew caught up with me. He had no mittens covering his cold, chapped hands.

"My mom won't let me go out without mittens," I exclaimed proudly.

"I don't have a mom," was the reply.

"My dad wouldn't either," I said.

"I don't have a dad," was his answer.

That evening was the first night of Hanukkah at my home. We'd retell the story of how enemies of the Jews had defiled all the oil needed to light the ancient temple, except for one cruse. The oil it contained should have burned for one day, but lasted for eight.

In remembrance of this long ago miracle, we'd light candles on eight nights. My brother, Mark, and I looked forward to the repetition of this ceremony and to reciting the Hebrew prayers and songs we'd learned. Before it began, we could smell the aroma of the delicious, crispy potato pancakes awaiting us. We also anticipated our gifts—Hanukkah *gelt*—chocolate rounds wrapped as gold coins.

After the ceremony, we sat down to dinner. It was then I said that I'd met a kid who didn't have a ma or a pa. Father said, without further comment, "A child like that is called an orphan."

Next morning, before leaving for school, Mother noticed my

mittens were missing. "Where are your mittens?" she asked.

I shrugged my shoulders. She waited for an answer.

"I lost them," I said.

"Why didn't you tell me sooner?"

Mother rushed from the vestibule and returned with another long woolen pair, which she carefully pinned to my parka with safety pins.

After school that day, I ran out, hoping to spot my new friend. As soon as I did, I blurted, "I know what you are, you are an orphan. My dad told me."

"That's right," he answered, "and if you come with me I'll show you another one."

I ran with him until we caught up with a slightly taller, thin, blue-eyed boy. My friend said, "This is Joel. His bed is next to mine at the orphanage."

I had frequently passed by the orphanage, but I hadn't known it. It was a large brick building with bars on all the windows, which I'd guessed was a prison.

"Joel, do you think we could sneak him in for a peek?"

Joel considered this and decided, "If we sneak him through the janitor's door!"

We went through a dark corridor, leading to some steps going up a narrow passageway. We stopped and listened. Not a sound. We opened the door into a long chamber, larger than a classroom. On both sides of the room were lines of beds. At the foot of each bed was a small, covered wooden box.

"What's in those boxes?" I asked.

How far that little candle throws his beams!
So shines a good deed in a naughty world.
—William Shakespeare

"Our clothes."

"Where do you eat?"

"In a big room upstairs, where there are long tables and benches, and we have to be quiet or our food is taken away."

I was late getting home. As my mother helped take off my parka, she noted that the mittens were gone, but the safety pins were intact.

She kneeled down to face me. "The mittens?"

I hung my head low. "I think I lost them again."

Mother lifted my chin. "You mean they were torn from the safety pins by somebody?"

I could not lie again. "The orphans have no money to buy mittens," I explained.

Before sundown, Mark and I each lit one Hanukkah candle.

After that evening, our Hannukah celebration was a little different.

My parents made arrangements with the orphanage directors for a different group of orphans to join us each night until all had joined us for the Festival of Lights. My parents also added entertainments for the parties.

The event everybody liked most featured lantern-slide projections of distant Africa—wild animals such as tigers, lions, giraffes, elephants, gorillas, hippopotamuses, all in their native habitat. "Oohs" and "aahs" of delight filled the room with each color slide.

At the end of each evening, every child received a gift of Hanukkah *gelt* and winter mittens.

Manuel E. Kadish is a retired physician who lives in Norwich, Connecticut. He is a Rotary Club member whose hobbies include skiing, photography and gardening.

SIX-POINTED STAR

Beth Aviv Greenbaum

We were Jews who celebrated Christmas—
a tree, lights, presents, the whole shebang.
Even my grandmother strung colored bulbs
around her windows: reds, oranges, whites, blues, greens.
We were German Jews, Americans like everyone else—

except my friends at school who got presents
for eight days: new sweaters, dolls, plastic horses,
books and necklaces with Jewish stars made
of gold, silver, rhinestones and cut glass.
I wanted a Jewish star. In kindergarten I learned

to draw a five-pointed star: make an "A"
with a long crossing line, connect that line
to each of the legs. But how to make a six-pointed star?
My friends knew: Make a triangle,
then another upside down on top of the first.

I wanted to wear a star. My father said, "No.
Jews had to wear stars in Europe. We're American.
No one has to know we're Jews. They did bad things
to Jews in Europe during the Second World War."
Then, for the first time, a tin menorah—

free from Sunday school—and candles:
pink, blue, yellow, white, red. I held
swirled wax between my thumb and fingers
and lit candles every night until eight burned—
gold light flickering in our living room.

Then a gift, a small white box from my father:
Inside on a thin cotton pillow, a gold chain
with a tiny gold star, no bigger
than my baby fingernail. How I loved that star
that draped my neck. I was like everyone else.

Beth Aviv Greenbaum lives in Michigan. She is the author of
Bearing Witness: Teaching the Holocaust *(Heinemann).*

FROSTY AND THE LOST BOY
Marilyn A. Mortenson-Cron

'O' nly half an hour," I muttered to myself as I headed for the mall that slushy pre-Christmas evening. My mission: find a pair of pants for our younger son to wear the next night for the Christmas program, and then I was out of there.

I joined the crowd streaming from the parking lot toward the mall's twinkling lights. Brushing past a bouncy, chattering, tow-headed munchkin with his dad, mom and grandma, I smiled at the child's exuberance, then put my blinders in place so as not to waste time.

I marched toward the boys' department, thinking of all I had yet to do that night. I resigned myself to it being near midnight by the time I finished correcting my students' papers—everything was so chaotic this time of year. No matter what, I was going to be home for snuggle time on the couch with my own two sons. I'd promised them we could watch a seasonal favorite, "Frosty the Snowman," on television.

Two, not one, pairs of pants were neatly tucked in the bag under my arm as I made my way toward the department store exit. I fumbled in my purse for my keys as I stepped down the crowded aisles. Not a second to waste.

A hand tugged my coat sleeve, and I heard a shaky voice ask, "Excuse me, I know you came in from the parking lot with us. This is silly, but have you seen our little boy?"

It was the older woman I'd seen in the entrance. The younger woman was beside her, her eyes frantically scanning the mall's central hall. "He has blonde hair," said the grandma, "and is about this tall." Grandma floated her hand to a level below my waist. "And he has a brown parka on. His name is Ryan."

"No, sorry, haven't seen him," I said, going on my way.

> *Heap on more wood!—the wind is chill!*
> *But let it whistle as it will,*
> *We'll keep our Christmas merry still.*
> —Sir Walter Scott

Why did I turn around? The younger woman's quivering lips? She must have been the mom. Or had the grandmother's misty tone just registered late with me? Maybe it was the fact I suddenly realized that the "Frosty the Snowman" song was playing throughout the mall.

I don't know why I turned and walked back, why it suddenly seemed that my time was not so precious. "Well, who have you asked for help?" I asked. "Is anyone else in the store looking? I haven't heard a thing announced over the loudspeakers."

"I spoke to one saleslady, who said she'd get it announced," the mother said. "I'm not sure what else to do. My husband is looking everywhere."

I noticed two other shoppers listening to our conversation, so I enlisted their help. Each walked in a different direction in search of Ryan. I asked a saleswoman to page the manager for us.

He appeared quickly, heard the problem, then sped to his office where he interrupted "Frosty" with a request that all be on the lookout for Ryan.

I remembered the mall's toy store—that would catch the eye of a wandering youngster—and strode off. "Well, yes," the toy store's teenage clerk said. "I did see a little boy dressed like that in here about ten or fifteen minutes ago. He headed for the back of the store."

I searched the store. No Ryan.

I headed back to his mother and grandmother. I could hear their calls, "Ryan, Ryan, where are you?" get louder as I hurried toward them. Ryan's mom said her husband had now gone off to check the men's rooms. I thought a second, then said I wanted to check out the entrance to the western-gear store, which boasted a life-size horse model.

I passed other shops en route; in each I could hear calls for Ryan. Yet if Ryan had discovered the mall's version of the Wild West, no one had found him there. I headed back to the department store entrance, where Ryan's relatives were. By now, the mall echoed with a chorus of calls for Ryan, and I probably wasn't needed. I felt the tug of my home, but it didn't feel right to leave before the little boy was found.

I stood with Ryan's mother and grandmother. Surrounded as we were with well-wishers calling out "Ryan," we rested our own voices and tried to think of a next step. We were staring straight out the mall entrance when the father appeared, Ryan's hand firmly in his.

Joy is a strange emotion, one that is usually felt. But I *saw* joy that night on the faces of Ryan and his family. The grown-ups thanked me; they didn't need to—seeing them rejoined with their little boy was enough.

At home, my own sleeping sons were curled on the couch with my husband. He disentangled himself slowly from their arms and rose to hug me, then asked, "Where have you been? You missed 'Frosty.' "

"No, I didn't miss 'Frosty,' " I answered. "Let me tell you why."

Marilyn A. Mortenson-Cron is a middle-school literacy teacher in Great Falls, Montana. She and her husband are members of the Gold Wing Road Riders Association.

I LOVE YOU, SANTA

John Harrington Burns

T o me, the first sign of Christmas is watching the window dressers change the world from Thanksgiving's orange and rust to the red and green of Christmas dreams. As December ripens, I enjoy the astonishment on the faces of children standing in line to meet Santa Claus.

Last Christmas, I was just settling myself down on my favorite bench, not too near and not too far from Santa's throne, when I received a sharp jolt to my right arm.

"Hey, mister. What's your name?"

I was annoyed. I just kept staring straight ahead at the children in line. Without bothering to turn, I answered the question with a question. "What's your name?"

"John," the voice replied.

I turned to tell the annoying John to stop poking and asking questions. But the words died. Sitting beside me was a smiling young man, whose beard was just beginning to shadow his complexion. He wore the same expression of awe as those children waiting to tell Santa their Christmas wishes.

John was an adolescent, destined to reach manhood and yet always have the innocent trust of a young child.

I smiled at him and winked the way old men do when they don't know what to say to a youngster.

John tried to wink back. He smiled and reached over to stroke my beard.

I pulled away.

"You have a white mustache and white beard, just like Santa Claus."

"Yes, that's true, but . . ."

"You're Santa Claus! I know it."

"Shrine of St. Nicholas; We are all good children." *by* Thomas Nast, 1862

The boy believed with all his heart that I was Santa Claus.

"Remember I wrote you a letter and asked you for the game where you push the red button and the puppy talks to you?"

"John, let me explain. I'm not who you think I am. Santa Claus is up there." I pointed to the nearby jovial man with the fake beard I'd sat down to watch.

"No. That's one of his helpers. My mom told me."

I was caught between two worlds, John's and mine. I struggled to find a way to end this conversation.

"If your Mom and Dad said you could have that toy, I'm sure you will find it under your Christmas tree on Christmas morning."

"Here comes my mom, now," he said.

Before he rose, John embraced this old man and said, "I love you, Santa."

"I love you too, John," I replied. And it was true.

Following World War II service aboard the USS Medrick AMc203, a wooden-hulled ship chasing derelict mines, John Harrington Burns was the lead singer of Four Jacks and A Jill. Retired from IBM, he is Director of the Freedom Museum and host of a cable TV show. He and his wife reside in Manassas, Virginia.

BOGART'S ANGEL

Gary Anderson

I look for miracles, especially at Christmas time. You know, those odd, wonderful happenings that become treasures of the memory simply because they can never be explained logically. One Christmas, I witnessed such a miracle, involving my dog, Bogart.

My children were very small that Christmas. As always, we set up our tree in the corner of the living room in our century-old farmhouse. And since Christmas lights and tinsel are a source of constant amazement to little ones, it was nearly a full-time job trying to keep them from accidentally pulling down the tree.

As if to come to my aid, Bogart began curling up in front of the tree, gently discouraging tiny hands from reaching for the branches by pushing them away with his nose. No matter how much my son and daughter tried, Bogart foiled their every effort to touch the tree.

Then one day, for no apparent reason, the dog began to show an affinity for an ornament on the tree. It was nothing special, just a small red-and-white striped angel, stuffed with cotton, sporting tinfoil wings of gold. Bogart could not take his eyes off that angel. He sat for hours, gazing at it. He nudged it with his nose and watched as it gently swung back and forth on its branch. He softly nipped at its tiny feet. He licked it. And most amazing of all, he cocked his head and listened intently, as if the angel were whispering to him.

It amused me to watch the dog and try to imagine what was going through his brain as he communed with his friend on our Christmas tree. Eventually, my kids rebelled; they thought it was unfair for the dog to be able to play with an ornament when they weren't allowed to pull on the light cords or eat the tinsel. So

 whenever I spied Bogart touching the angel, I scolded or whacked him on the nose.

Bogart continued to nudge his angel whenever he thought I wasn't looking. One afternoon, I walked into the living room after having put the kids down for their naps. While I'd been gone, Bogart had removed his angel from the tree and was now lying by the fireplace, gently chewing on her foot. He wasn't doing any real damage, but it was definitely something I couldn't allow.

After I'd reprimanded him and rescued the ornament, Bogart followed me back to the Christmas tree. This time I hung the angel well out of his reach.

For the rest of that Christmas season, Bogart sat at the tree base, sniffing the spot where his little angel had been, then simply looking up at her on her new perch. He couldn't reach her—didn't even try—but there was still something going on between the two of them. As I watched him during the still, frosty nights, I got the feeling that there was an aura about the whole thing that was almost, well . . . holy.

Maybe you can explain how an affinity could develop between a dog and a Christmas angel, but I can't. Bogart's fascination remains a mystery—a gift I can never unwrap. And after all, isn't that really what Christmas is all about—the celebration of events we can never fully comprehend?

Gary Anderson raised two children as a single parent. Since 1996 he has written a family-oriented humor column for Iowa's largest-circulation rural monthly. He is the author of the short story collection, Spider's Night on the Broom *(Writers Club Press).*

ALSO IN THIS SERIES

FORTITUDE

True Stories of True Grit

EDITED BY MALINDA TEEL

"*Fortitude's* plainspoken, honest narratives of remarkable eloquence will remind you of the great chronicles of Studs Terkel."
— *Inside/Outside Magazine*

"Like gapers on the highway, readers want to know how these ordinary people manage to display true grit when faced with insurmountable obstacles."
—*Booklist*

"This outstanding anthology is often humorous, frequently inspiring, always compelling and highly recommended to anyone who appreciates stories of human courage in adversity, ingenuity in difficulty, and perseverance in hardship."
—*Internet Book Watch*

"An inspiration for taking life at full force" 　　—*Nashville News*

COMING SOON

HOPE: True Stories of Dreams Fulfilled

WISDOM: True Stories of Life's Lessons

ALSO AHEAD

FAITH: True Stories of Friendship, Principle and Belief

JUSTICE: True Stories of Fair Play

Visit us at www.VirtueVictorious.com.